# The Steering Wheel

## Caroline Anne Butt

The Steering Wheel
ISBN paperback 978 1 76109 917 5
ISBN ebook 978 1 76109 918 2
Copyright © text Caroline Anne Butt 2025
Cover image by Graham Davidson
Some names have been changed.

First published 2025 by
**GINNINDERRA PRESS**
PO Box 2 Bentleigh 3204
ginninderrapress.com.au

"Intelligently and brilliantly crafted, this poignant story chronicles one woman's journey through the 70s and 80s as she confronts deeply ingrained societal expectations of both men and women. It explores her courageous struggle to overcome physical challenges, navigate the fear of judgment from family and friends, and face the complexities of a troubled marriage. Ultimately, it's a moving account of her fight to discover her true inner strength and create a safe, peaceful haven for herself and her children."

Lorraine D. Corne<br>Consulting Psychologist'

'The luminous power of Butt's writing, her delightful ironic humour and insatiable curiosity, lifts a harrowing story into one of resilience, courage and hope.'

Karen Whitelaw,<br>Writer, Teacher and Editor

*I dedicate this memoir to my parents - Stan and Ruby,
to my children - Paul and Rebecca,
to my grandsons - Jade, Sage (dec), Samson, Sonny, Eddison,
and to my extended family and friends.*

# Contents

| | |
|---|---|
| The Up Down Spin Around Line | 7 |
| Pandora's Box | 19 |
| Snail Mail | 30 |
| Gaytime Caravan Park | 41 |
| The Class Warrior | 48 |
| First Home | 55 |
| Mould | 61 |
| The School Fete | 68 |
| A Real Treat | 74 |
| Stirrups | 80 |
| The Right Order | 87 |
| Life and Death | 94 |
| The Arrival | 101 |
| Happy Nappy Valley | 107 |
| Guilty Pleasure | 115 |
| The Spire | 122 |
| Weak Ankles | 128 |
| CVA | 138 |
| Step by Step | 145 |
| No Looking Back | 150 |
| Painting White Roses | 157 |
| A Daughter of Eve | 166 |
| Sick Leave | 175 |
| The Immolation | 180 |
| The Social Worker | 190 |
| A Reasonable Man | 195 |
| Faultlines | 201 |
| Afterword | 208 |
| Acknowledgements | 215 |

# The Up Down Spin Around Line

It was the first time as a passenger in my own car when I didn't know where I was going. The only clue I had didn't bode well. I'd overheard Thomas telling Mum on the quiet that we were headed interstate, for the Barossa Valley. It was the first day of our honeymoon and as Thomas pulled away from the motel I felt a pit in my stomach.

Weeks earlier he'd asked, 'Where would you like to go?'

'The beach. I'd love to have some time there.'

I needed to get in sync with a slow-moving tide. It'd give us a chance to ground ourselves after the manic year I'd had and the lead up to the wedding. I imagined we'd stroll hand in hand along the water's edge. We'd fall into champagne sands and watch salmon sunsets.

'How about you? What would you like to do?'

'I'd like to do some travelling.'

So we agreed – a few days at the beach followed by travelling.

I often enquired about the arrangements expecting to be involved in the planning, but Thomas would say, 'It's a surprise.'

As we drove away from the motel that morning, I wondered which beach we'd head for but by mid morning Thomas had driven well away from the coast.

'Where are we going?'

'It's a surprise.'

We travelled into familiar territory - the Southern Highlands, where I'd once taught. I was surprised when we pulled up outside one of the groomsmen's homes. His wife, Kathy, the local librarian, had been very kind to me when I lived down there. She hadn't been able to come to the wedding because their first child was due any day. Greg, a keen train enthusiast like Thomas, and Kathy, hosted a delicious morning tea. So, yes, catching up with them was a pleasant surprise and everyone seemed to be aware that we were running to a timetable so we shunted off and headed further south.

'Where are we off to?'

Thomas laughed. He liked this game but, for me, its novelty had worn off. My sense of direction was towards breaking waves. A directional pull had my whole being reaching out for a smiling beach.

It was late lunchtime when we pulled up outside an impressive looking house. We'd arrived in a leafy suburb in Canberra. We were at the home of a couple who'd recently returned from overseas because the wife had developed a terminal illness and needed to be nearer to family. Her husband was another of Thomas's lifelong friends. His wife, Ruth, who'd been too ill to travel down to our wedding had prepared a delicious salad and dessert.

Soon we were saying goodbye and headed further sou'west.

Thomas yawned a few times. He said, 'We're running late.'

'I can drive if you like.'

He chuckled. 'But you don't know where we're going.'

I knew where I wanted to go – to the coast – but I could see there was no sign of that. The last few crumbs of my weary body hoped that not too far away we could stop at a motel and fall onto a comfy bed.

All day I felt like that young child sitting in the back seat of my parents' car, for what seemed to be an interminable amount of time, waiting to arrive at one of Mr Hungerford's cottages. His cottages had been by the ocean at The Entrance on the Central Coast. Our family had a permanent month long booking there every year. That childlike feeling of will-we-ever-arrive swamped me. Someone, not my parents, this time my husband, was the only one who knew where we were going.

While we travelled sou'west, I realised that I'd left something dear behind – my autonomy. The honeymooner – that is the me who'd been dealing with months of busyness and responsibilities before the wedding – needed to sleep for a week in one of Mr Hungerford's cottages.

I didn't want to complain. I could see by Thomas's eagerness that he had a surprise in store. I didn't want to spoil it. I needed to be patient.

As we continued along the Snowy Mountains Highway, I stared up into the starstruck night. 'Are we nearly there?'

'We'll get tea soon.'

By the time we arrived in Cooma, the sun had long set and all shops had shut.

Thomas was annoyed. 'You'd think there'd be something open. I know it's late but-'

That was an understatement. It was ridiculously late. There seemed to be no boundary to this day. As we climbed in altitude, I wouldn't have been surprised if at any moment we'd have arrived at the Mount Kosciusko summit to meet up with another rail enthusiast and his wife, for supper.

I've forgotten the name of the place where we stayed on our first night. No-one was there to greet us. All lights were off. It was so dark we could hardly find the chalet let alone the key and its keyhole. It was one of a cluster of faux chalets designed to get travellers in the mood for the Snowy.

After I made us a cup of tea and we shared the motel's rationed biscuits, I fell into bed while Thomas paced backwards and forwards.

'Are you okay?'

He didn't answer. I soon learnt that this was his night time ritual – to pace and throw the emotions of the day into a big pot then stir and stir. It reminded me of the witches' words in Macbeth –'double, double, toil and trouble.' When his pacing stopped, Thomas took something out of his port and climbed into bed and opened it.

I said, 'What's that?'

'It's the itinerary.'

It was neatly printed and filled a whole page.

'May I have a look?'

He pulled away. He wouldn't have done that had he'd known about my map reading skills as a navigator on a couple of fun amateur car trials. With the driver's skill and my navigator's skill, interpreting all maps upside down, we came first a couple of times. This groom had no idea how lucky he was.

I kept my hand out even though I could see he was reluctant to hand it over. I laughed, thinking he was playing with me, but he huffed and puffed. I realised he wasn't playing but it was important for me to stand up for my person. It was like I'd asked him to hand over his very soul.

'Thomas, I like to know where I'm going.' I read the itinerary. 'It says there are fourteen nights at different motels.'

'Charlie said you get two nights free that way.'

'Does that mean we're travelling every day?'

'We need an early start in the morning.'

'But, it's not what we – I mean we're –'

'There are two nights at Phillip Island.'

'Where's that?' I looked it up. It was a week away. 'Can we cancel some of these, please? Can we have a couple of nights in the same place?'

"No. I've paid for everything upfront.'

'I wish I'd known.'

In this watershed moment, I felt unsure of my ground. I'd been so looking forward to having a few relaxing days. Did I have any right to ask him to change the itinerary?

As if reading my mind, he said, 'It's too late to change anything.' Thomas kissed me good night, turned off his bed lamp and as he rolled away he said, 'Remember, it's an early start in the morning.' He fell asleep straight away.

I didn't. I was more awake than I'd been all day. Thomas might have felt he was heading in the right direction but I wasn't. I needed to stop now, not in a week's time. I couldn't believe how the itinerary showed brazen disregard for what we'd discussed.

Cold blood ran through my veins. I pulled up the blankets and curled into a ball. This was nothing like I'd expected.

In the next few days, I'd discover the scale and sheer audacity of the travel plans. Of course, the budding wife in me excused the groom's enthusiasm. Perhaps it'd been a misunderstanding. It was more bearable to think like that than to see it for what it was. I'd been duped. If our marriage had been a material object I would've returned it in the first twenty four hours and asked for a full refund.

I turned off the bed lamp and tried not to think or to feel but my gut screamed. I didn't know then that while it communicated with my main brain it was an all important second brain. Instead, I chided myself. 'Get a grip, girl. It's early days – calm down.'

In the morning, we packed our things and I determined to make the most of the new day. Because of the obvious shift in Thomas's demeanour since we'd married, I was more conscious of the political space in which we moved.

We were an official microcosm of society: husband and wife. We entered into a lawful union and it wasn't just about us. It was also about being part of the fabric of our community, our society and its greater good. I'd promised to love and care for my husband who was already giving me the impression that when he spoke it wasn't to me, it was to someone else.

Our courtship had been the opposite and I couldn't believe how quickly his priotities had shifted. Hopefully, it was a temporary glitch. I figured that in Thomas's mind he wasn't doing anything wrong. He simply assumed charge as countless married men had done down centuries. Some men, of course, would've shown more interest in their wives whereas Thomas seemed preoccupied. Often when I spoke to him he didn't answer.

True to his word, and bound by the hidden demands of Thomas's agenda, we started out early. Our first stop was Thredbo. We caught a chairlift to the top of the mountain and back again. It was fun looking down onto the sparkling white ocean of snow beneath. It was breathtaking. Sturdy snow gums spread their long sensuous lines of purple shadows onto the sunlit canvas. I vowed to come back sometime and paint them.

As we drove into the third and fourth new town, I recognised a pattern. Instead of driving up the main street, Thomas would slow down and look to the left and right.

'What are you looking for?'

'A station.'

He subsequently found and photographed every railway line, railway station, stationmaster's cottage and goods shed in existence.

At this point, he'd park the car and hurry off to get a photo spot. Thomas was a keen photographer and a very good one. Some of his photos were used on front covers of enthusiasts' books and in rail magazines and accompanied some of his published articles. He'd scoot off to wherever while I investigated the old sandstone buildings.

I'd stand on an 1890s platform and go back in time and imagine how busy the platform must've been in its heyday; men in top hats, in suits with fob watches glittering on waistcoats and women in long skirts, gloves, laced-up shoes and designer hats.

With each new rail platform or goods yard, my indignation rose. I couldn't believe the tightness of the schedule. We were always hurrying from A to B with no time allocated for pottering or for spotting a bookshop or local art gallery.

I made a request. 'Thomas, I'd like to see the main street of every town before you branch off to the railway station. I need to get a sense of where I am.'

He was offended by my insinuation. 'You're seeing the best of everything.'

'I enjoyed the chairlift but that was days ago. All I'm seeing now are train things and it's too hot for me to stand in the sun while you go off and take photos.'

As we came into the next town, Thomas obliged my request, literally. He drove up and down the town's main street.

'For Your Information This is The Main Street.'

I ignored his condescension. 'Thank you. I appreciate that. Can we stop and have a look around?'

'We don't have time.'

At that juncture, I was unaware that Thomas and Charlie, his best man and best mate, had drawn up a tight schedule, so tight it didn't allow for late running. Trains often ran late, which meant Thomas was always trying to make up time to meet the next planned photo stop.

'We have to keep moving.'

I was an unsettled and genuinely unhappy Vegemite but as an apprentice wife, I knew my lines. I smiled and acquiesced. I believed that in time we'd grow closer together and we'd learn to listen to each other's needs. All I needed now was patience. We were a work in progress, just like everyone else, or so I thought.

I was often uncomfortable at the speed at which Thomas drove, and he barely watched the road. He looked out more for things off road than on road, especially if we travelled parallel to a railway line. As we raced between each town, I was on full alert.

One morning as we drove west to goodness-knows-where, the car wheels skidded into gravel and pulled up close to a bridge.

Thomas jumped out. 'Take these will you? The train's due any minute.' Thomas pointed to two cameras. He hurried onto the bridge to check out the best photo spot.

I called out, 'Do you want me to take a photo with one of them?'

At this point, I was prepared to do anything to distract myself from the fright I'd just had when we'd skidded in the loose gravel. For a minute, I thought Thomas had lost control of the car. One of the cameras was a complicated German one, so I chose the simpler automatic and handed him the other one.

Thomas waved it away. 'No, no, it's all right. It's all right.' He reached for the camera I held in my hand. 'You take mine.'

'What do you mean?'

'This one's Charlie's.'

My increasing suspicion had been right. I couldn't look at Thomas. This was no honeymoon. This was Thomas and Charlie's personal indulgence, a boys' own adventure, a trainspotters' fest.

I froze with disappointment in the midday heat. I took a few deep breaths to calm my thumping heart while Thomas pointed to where he wanted me to stand.

As we stood on the overhead bridge, I heard a train coming, coming, coming, clickety-clack, clickety-clack. When it roared into view, I pressed the button and heard the solid click of the lens. I'd just exposed an upside-down-spin-around moment in my life.

The train driver blew the diesel's powerful horn at us before disappearing under the rail bridge. Thomas raced to the other side and took more photos. I didn't. I couldn't. I was nailed to the spot. My hope had been ripped from me.

Thomas smiled as he hurried back. 'That was great – thought I'd missed it. C'mon, sweetheart. Let's go.'

At this point, I didn't care whether he thought he'd missed the train or not. I was the one who'd missed something. My heart belted against my chest. I puffed in the heat as I walked back to the car. I wouldn't have had any objection to a few train spotting days, but this? It was madness and an insult to my person.

When Thomas drove back onto the main road, it was midday and my head pounded from the heat. We travelled directly into the sun for hours.

Thomas always had control of the steering wheel because, as he said, he was the only one who knew where we were going. Whenever I offered to drive, he reacted as if I'd stamped on his manhood.

We reached Swan Hill after a long hot stretch. Thomas said he wanted to check out a particular museum. I excused myself. I had an urgent need. I suspected I had a chill in the bladder, though I didn't know why.

I found a single out-of-date lavatory outside the museum and couldn't wait to get in out of the sun. When I opened the door, an overwhelming acrid smell escaped from a desperately-needed-to-be-cleaned loo. I coughed, stepped back and shut the door. No words would do justice to the condition of the toilet seat or the floor, where a chorus of dung-eating blowflies multiplied.

Over the next few days, whenever we stopped, my priority was to find shade and a clean ladies' loo. I couldn't stand behind a tree and relieve myself like Thomas. By now, I was pissed off in more ways than one. Whenever possible, I'd stay in the shade of the loo or under a tree to escape the heat while Thomas took photos. I also tried to cope with an increasingly painful urge to pee.

My body mirrored the ache in the landscape. Heat shimmered off the backs of sun-struck cattle. Forlorn sheep roasted in shadeless dehydrated paddocks. And Thomas was still expecting me to accept the serendipity of the trip.

"Oh, look, sweetheart, we're just in time to catch the ABC123 KPD693 on the up-down inside-out line.'

That's not exactly what he said, but it sounded like it to me. It was Thomas spinning lines and his moods depended on whether the trains ran on time. If, for example, Thomas the Tank Engine, or one of his mates, ran late, Thomas would take it personally.

How I wished I was brave enough to take the keys and turn the car around and head east, where I could rely on sunrises kissing the Pacific. If Thomas didn't want to come, he didn't have to. But, of course, it was my fantasy, in a fragile, isolated atmosphere, in the middle of nowhere.

My disappointments simmered like mini mirages just like the ones up ahead shimmying off the asphalt on the long stretch of road. This honeymoon was the biggest mirage of all.

Thomas continued to feign surprise whenever we happened to stumble across another abandoned line or happened to be just in time to see a particular train on the main line. More photo stops; always more photo stops.

My increasing resentment could have ripped up the nearest rail line but weariness took over. My main goal for each day was to tread warily, to keep the temperature down inside the car by faking interest knowing that this train-fest would soon end.

One morning, we left a motel from heaven-knows-where and drove to a small southern town near an early settlers' fishing bay snuggled into the landscape. Thomas drove back and forth, back and forth.

'What are you looking for?'

'For an old embankment – an abandoned line.'

I startled when Thomas braked and did another unexpected U-turn. And another. He slammed the brakes and smacked and smacked the steering wheel which had never been smacked before. He jumped out of the car, opened the boot and disappeared.

I lent across and patted the steering wheel. I'd never witnessed an outburst like this by anyone. I shrank back and tried to become as inanimate as my seat but I soon faded in the heat so had to get out. I stood back on the side of the road. It was a desolate place, more desolate than the middle of nowhere. It wasn't like I could say, 'Look, this isn't working for me.'

Thomas scanned the pages of the books frantically. 'I don't have time for this.'

I was surprised he'd brought so many books with him. I'd deliberately not packed any because I assumed that at times we'd walk along an unknown street in an unknown town and spy a bookshop, as you do. We'd wander in and linger and I'd find a surprise or two. Unfortunately, abandoned railway stations didn't sell books.

I stood beside Thomas in the scorching heat and felt a sense of disconnection from everything around me and realised I was sick. Apart from the constant urge to find a loo, I'd developed a fever.

Out of sheer desperation, and to settle a frustrated Thomas, I threw my undeveloped surveying skills into action and unexpectedly uncovered the location of the abandoned line. It was disguised by the presence of an abandoned tennis court on the same site. It was a case of lateral thinking and layered history. Mission accomplished.

As we drove out of town, I felt as if I'd been filleted and bled back into the bay.

Another motel. Another restaurant where evening wine quenched Thomas's thirst and increased his verbosity. We sat beside a large window overlooking the pool. Thomas recalled the days events as if to someone else – probably Charlie – and I was the dry run. Although we sat close together we were far apart. He relived the day while I waited for it to start.

By now, I felt so unwell I had an urge to flee or go mad. To protect myself from rising panic, I looked out the window hoping to connect with something. Anything. I needed to connect now. Yes –the hibiscus – that was it – check out its highlights – what colour might I use for the first wash? I gazed at the sparkles on the pool; mirrored starlight dancing. I listened to the playful laughter of a family in the pool. I followed the ripples on the surface until I became its lap-lap lap-lap.

I turned and as I watched Thomas empty his plate, I felt a presence.

It was loneliness wrapping itself around me, and it soon became my faithful companion. At least, it recognised me. That was more than I could say for Thomas. He made me feel I was about as necessary as yesterday's newspaper.

On our last leg home, he wanted to explore an historic site in a village which had once been a whaling port. I wanted to walk along the beach but felt too uncomfortable. My fever was worse. I could no longer blame the heat.

Thomas went on his way while I searched the main street for a chemist. I explained my symptoms to the pharmacist and her first question was, 'Are you on your honeymoon?'

How did she know? Was it the shine on my new wedding ring?

She proceeded to tell me about the honeymooner's uterine infection. She said she'd make up a concoction which would give me instant relief, and it did.

We didn't chase trains on that day. After the museum stop, we headed for home. We unpacked the car and climbed the stairs to our first floor unit in the welcoming cool old double-brick building in Penshurst Street, Willoughby.

Thomas unlocked the door. He turned and, with a flourish, picked me up and carried me over the threshold. 'There,' he said, 'just like in the movies.'

He placed me down in the small foyer. I glanced at our reflection in the hallstand's oval mirror and hardly recognised the startled, wide-eyed wife looking back at me.

# Pandora's Box

After we moved into our spacious first-floor unit, Thomas said one night as we ate dinner, 'There's a branch line closing down out west. Charlie and I are going on its last ride.'

'When?'

'Tomorrow. We'll leave after work.'

As a very new wife, I wasn't too sure how to handle this last-minute news. We'd only been back from our honeymoon a month and money was tight.

'Shouldn't we have discussed this first? I mean, can we afford it?'

Thomas shrugged. 'Charlie said he'll help if -'

'There'll be more closures in the future, won't there? It's just-'

By now, I'd learnt some rail jargon, much to Thomas's chagrin.

He barely spoke during dinner, which said to me that I'd spoken out of turn. Later that night, in bed, he lobbied. 'I have to go on this trip, sweetheart.' He cuddled up. 'It's the last run before it closes; a once in a lifetime chance.'

After we said our goodnights, we rolled away from each other, leaving a noticeable chill between us. I'd been surprised by our lack of intimacy: rare chatting, little affection. I'd expected it to grow. I liked being referred to as Thomas's wife and I liked referring to him as my husband; a boastful part of a bride's vocabulary; a societal proclamation which vibrated status and security. And there were the titles - Mr and Mrs. It was as if the title lifted us up into a higher echelon of society. It assumed it was where the adults lived; where the passing on of DNA took place; Jane Austen territory; Emma looking over my shoulder.

The next afternoon, Thomas swapped his briefcase for his small travel bag and kissed me goodbye. 'You know, I'd feel happier if you'd stay with your parents while I'm away.'

'Why?'

'I'm worried about the neighbours.'

'The neighbours are fine.'

'What if downstairs have another party? It'd be better if you stay with your parents.'

'I'm not a little girl."

Thomas opened the front door and turned and kissed me. I stood at the top of the stairs and watched as he jumped them, two at a time and his resonant tenor voice echoed in the empty stairwell when he called out, 'I love you, sweetheart. Love you. I'll miss you. Bye.'

It was so loud I felt embarrassed. This wasn't the first time there'd been a purposeful display. They always confused me because, for some reason, I felt diminished. It was the same when he'd posture holding hands in public or when he'd lean across and, unexpectantly, kiss me in front of others. I couldn't orientate myself. Our life in the public domain was so different to our private life. I was always correcting the two different readings and trying to realign my compass to true north.

Now that I was living with Thomas, I'd begun to read him for the first time behind closed doors. I was beginning to read his patterns and mannerisms. He was an excellent actor. I supposed his years of singing training helped. I hadn't noticed any of these things during our courtship. I can't say I liked my tendency to have niggling doubts about our relationship. I'd noticed when Thomas was in the company of certain friends, he looked truly happy.

I closed the front door and walked across to the first-floor window to wave and watch them drive away. I shook off the pressing thoughts. As

Mum always said, 'There you go - being too analytical.' It wasn't that. It was that I'd been taught from the pulpit not to trust my own emotions. Apparently, they were unreliable. But, often, I'd wonder about the public and private Thomas.

At the window, my unravelling self pulled back the lace curtain and watched Charlie take Thomas's bag and pack it into the boot.

It was late afternoon and peak-hour traffic zoomed close by as they hopped into the car. Penshurst Street was now a busy artery. I'd lived on it for the first nineteen years of my life on the same side of the street at 68, just a few blocks down, but it was a much busier road now. The units were double brick and set well back. There was a low brick fence which attempted to restrain nondescript bushes.

Thomas and Charlie chatted oblivious to me standing at the window waiting to wave goodbye. When they pulled away, I felt a pang when I saw Charlie's hands on the steering wheel.

I turned back and looked at the living room. This was my life now. At least, I could look forward to having some quiet time to myself.

It was a good time to go down to the front garden and pick some late blooming hydrangeas and greenery. I filled a large urn with colour, texture and line and set them up in the corner of the sou'east windows. It was a perfect setting for generous wedding gifts: a large vase and a small faux Queen Anne side table. I stood back and admired the arrangement. I'd like to have said to Thomas, 'Isn't that beautiful?'

Before Thomas had walked out, he'd said, 'Seeing you're not going to stay with your parents you can unpack the rest of the boxes. That'll give you something to do.'

I was tempted to salute and bow down before him and say, 'Yes, Master,' but I didn't. The new wife in me knew it would be a bad idea and a touch disrespectful. Instead, I smiled and said, 'That's a good idea.'

It felt strange being organised into this junior role. The obscuration of me-being-me made my gut churn. Me-being-me sat in silence on the lounge near the last of the boxes, which contained double-and-triple-ups of electrical goods, vases and casserole dishes. I'd either have to give them away or open a shop.

In the cool stillness, I listened to the muffle and shuffle of other residents in the building. There was the lively chatter of the young couple downstairs as they did their weekly Friday night washing in the shared laundry outside.

The wife-in-me reminded myself I needed to unpack the boxes.

But I didn't want to. I was too tired. It'd been a busy week. It was time to sit back, put up my feet and relax. But where was Thomas? Where were his feet? I would have liked them beside mine. That's when I burst into tears. Thomas was always anywhere but here. I'd noticed that he always looked happier when he was walking out the door than when he walked in.

Thoughts and tears surfaced while I busied myself making a simple three-veg dinner for one. As I finished eating, the young woman from downstairs knocked on the door.

'We're having a get together tomorrow night. Would you like to come?'

I knew it was her polite way of giving notice. 'Thanks for asking but I'm already doing something. Have a great time.'

I was tempted to race off and stay at my parents because the music would be loud for hours but I wanted to stay home. Of course, I'd stay. This was my home now. Indirectly, I did attend the party. The next night, the Beach Boys' Good Vibrations rocked me to sleep sometime after midnight.

All tears had long gone by then. I'd given myself a good talking to and knew it was up to me to make the most of my situation. No two marriages would ever be the same. I could no longer project Mum and Dad's marriage onto ours.

I'd kidded myself when I'd thought that once upon a time they'd been just like us. It was a shock when I first realised that Thomas was no clone of my father's. It was my ingenious projection of Dad onto Thomas that got me to where I sat alone on this Friday night. Until my disappointing honeymoon, I'd never really had my belief in others tested but I was prepared to excuse it as an anomaly; that maybe Thomas had misunderstood.

Next morning, I unpacked boxes and stacked the rest of them into the small sunroom on the eastern side of the unit. It was a well lit small room which would make an excellent art studio. I imagined setting up the easel and not having to pack away my paints and brushes. I hadn't said anything to Thomas about it because, these days, I had no time to paint and Thomas had also mentioned the sunroom.

'I'd like to build a model railway board to fit it. Charlie and I built one years ago at Mum's.'

I'd never stepped inside the sunroom at his mother's place. It was a room where June would only partially open the door just wide enough to throw in art and craft and women's magazines she wanted to keep.

She said, 'One day I'm going to turn that room into an arts and crafts room.'

June was a beautiful craftswoman having been a tailor when young. She was still grieving the death of her husband, John, who'd died shortly before I met Thomas. She was semi-retired, so I offered to help her set up the sunroom. She appeared enthusiastic.

I said, 'If you like, we could make a day of it in the next school holidays.'

'I'd love that. Thank you, darling.'

The day came but at the last minute June rang. 'I've got a bowls' tournament today so don't worry. We can do it anytime. There's no hurry.'

June often put off things. Sometimes we'd arrive to find her curled up in her two-seater with the TV blaring. We could see she'd been crying.

I said to Thomas, 'Let's do the room anyway. It'll give her a lift.'

She'd repeatedly asked Thomas to move his things out, so we decided to do both things on the same day.

When Thomas opened the sunroom door, there was a beautiful burst of morning sunshine. In my mind, I'd imagined the room dark and forbidding but the quality of light through the eastern windows was perfect for an art and craft room.

I felt a wave of excitement for June. She could sit in here and lose herself in projects. She could look out onto the row of mature camellias she'd nurtured for years. They stood proudly alongside the side fence and lined the driveway.

To the left, there was a window in the northern wall which looked out over the back garden. The jacaranda was the leading lady with a mass of snowdrops at her feet. Maples and azaleas shaded the fish pond. Cumquats stood in large pots on either side of the back steps leading up to the patio, where there stood a treasured collection of bonsai beauties next to a growing pile of rubbish.

The sunroom was stacked ultra-high with boxes and piles of magazines. When we cleared it, I discovered a door which opened into the main bedroom. How lovely! June could now open up her bedroom door to a sunny morning corner of the house.

As I sorted magazines, I came across some of Thomas's paraphernalia. 'Thomas, can you help me move this?'

It was a large box sitting on top of magazines which were covered in dust and spider webs on what appeared to be a very large bench or a long table. As we moved magazines on top of the boxes, and the magazines under the boxes, there was a slow reveal. In this quiet suburban bungalow, in this quiet suburban sunroom, lay splintered remains.

It took a while to make sense of it. In its past life, it had been Thomas's model railway enthusiast's board, about two metres long by a metre wide. But, now, sharp pieces of board jutted out and hung loose.

The model railway lines were buckled. Hours of construction of model railway stations and houses were flattened. I looked at what was once the frontline of a war zone.

'What happened here?'

Thomas glanced in its direction. "Ah, yes, Not one of my finest moments.'

It looked like someone had taken to it with an axe.

'What happened?'

'I tried to demolish it. Didn't do a very good job, did I?'

'What do you mean?'All I could see was a swinging axe.'Dad kept telling me I was lazy. He spent hours out here so I-'

'Oh, Thomas. Your poor Dad.'

'It wasn't a very nice thing to do.'

My stomach churned. This was a major overreaction if ever there was one. It wasn't a simple red flag. This was at the level of Edvard Munch's *The Scream*. Each splintered board was victim and witness to the anger behind the felling of an axe.

I said, 'But you wouldn't have been able to use it either.'

'I hadn't used it for years. I used Charlie's.'

'It would've been terrifying.'

'Yeah. I feel bad about it now.' He shrugged.

I wanted to flee.

As I worked alongside Thomas, I told myself not to panic, but it didn't work. A core deep within me felt the tremor of the striking power of my husband's revenge. It was palpable; calculated terror at a vulnerable time for his parents.

His father's heart attacks and two strokes had changed their family dynamics. For Thomas to resort to this because he'd been asked to do more around the house was more than a concern.

Where were his parents at the time of his fury? I dared not ask. I wanted to cry for his stroke-ridden father, for the powerlessness and fear he must've felt in the midst of his grown son's retaliation, and about which his father would've had no control.

I felt the weight of an axe over me. I didn't want to believe that Thomas was responsible for something so ugly. It belonged in the movies, not real life. Years later, I read in John Denver's autobiography about how Annie, his ex-wife, had enraged him after their separation. He heard she'd cut down some trees on the property. They'd been his favourite trees so he went in and, I quote, 'got the power saw... cut off the corner of the kitchen table... cut up the dining table... descended on the bedroom... sawed the bedhead.' Denver sounded proud of his achievement. He made no mention of the terror he'd inflicted. His song lyrics, 'You fill up my senses' took on a whole new meaning.

When June arrived home later that afternoon, we showed her the restored sunroom. She put her head around the door then closed it quickly. My heart went out to her. I wanted to hug her and ask if she was okay but I felt that I'd done enough damage already. I'd unwillingly exposed a family secret, about the one whom she always referred to as her 'perfect son... who should've been a priest.'

June thanked us and within weeks the sunroom filled with clutter again. She pushed the chest of drawers up against the side door to her bedroom and stacked boxes on it.

Around this time, the lease on our flat was due to expire and I assumed we'd renew it. We'd recently bought land and the next step was to find a builder and get a quote. Around the same time, our minister rang and asked to speak to Thomas. He wondered if we'd consider being caretakers of a nearby home in Forestville, for a period of twelve months, while its owners were overseas.

Thomas sounded keen. 'I can't wait to get away from this place.'

Admittedly, there were the occasional noisy parties downstairs but the people in the building, and the building itself, were welcoming. Our unit had high ceilings and large rooms.

'I like it here and we're so close to everything.'

'Exactly. Too close for my liking.'

Being assertive with Thomas was difficult. If I expressed an opinion or stood up for my person, there'd be a sudden change in air pressure. It wasn't merely uncomfortable. It was like being in high humidity and like being caught in an air bubble before the storm.

The first signs were always Thomas's elbows. They'd dig into his sides whether sitting or standing, which made me wary. Not that I was worried about anything physical happening. It was more a case of - uh-oh- time to be quiet - and I'd become as mute as the paisley wallpaper.

If Thomas believed a tomato was a potato and I disagreed and said it was a tomato, because it was quite obviously a tomato, Thomas would become contrary.

I missed the goodwill fun we used to have with Mum and Dad around the dinner table, talking and laughing about, let's say, tomatoes and potatoes, and how alike or unalike they were. No one at the table was ever more right than anyone else. We'd have our say, regardless of how outlandish or ridiculous our points of view. I didn't know then how revealing our potato-tomato scenes were. They were actual fractals which revealed, to the more experienced eye, the essence of predictive patterns of behaviour.

Thomas went ahead and arranged for us to meet the owners of the rental house the following Saturday. The elderly couple were warm and friendly. Their house was a three bedroom weatherboard in a small cul-de-sac amongst other brick and weatherboard homes. The owners said they'd lock up one bedroom with their more precious goods.

The tall thin Swedish husband said, 'Make yourselves at home.'

The rent would be the same as the unit. His friendly wife took me around and pointed out a few things: the expensively framed oil paintings, some with their own small lamp, hanging on every wall. The French-polished dining setting;

'You can't leave a glass of water on the table. It'll leave a stain.'

The lounge suite with its two grand armchairs and matching antimacassars took centre stage in the living room. The plush carpet looked like it required regular maintenance. As I took in this information, I worried that we were novices in housekeeping and shouldn't be trusted to look after these treasures.

Inside the living room, a luscious ivy vine wound itself around the top of the large front window and along the room divide. I'd never looked after an indoor plant before. I hoped it was a survivor. Even the front garden was a concern. It was filled with white standard roses along the driveway and along the front of the property. We were expected to prune them while we lived there. This house and garden spelt Responsibility.

But there was an attraction. The husband was a theologian and author and he offered us the use of his ceiling-to-floor library in the third bedroom. The budding contemplative in me couldn't say no. What lay ahead would be a feast of philosophy, soul food and biography.

Their home was only a suburb away from where we'd recently bought land in the beautiful bush at Belrose; Guringal country. I imagined we'd visit it most weekends but we didn't, so sometimes I drove there after school. I'd stand in the afternoon sun and wonder about the best placement of house and garden. I imagined our modest Cape Cod fitting snugly into the end of the quiet tree-lined cul-de-sac.

We'd already agreed that the kitchen and bathroom tiles would be white with dark blue trim highlighted with warm yellow accessories. I had Monet's kitchen in mind, and imagined half the house with Monet as designer, but Thomas kept saying he wasn't too sure about builders.

'Builders aren't what they used to be.'

I lived on hope. I imagined our children playing in the filtered shade while we pottered in the garden. The block faced east-west. We could sit out the back of a late afternoon on a family-sized decking and have dinner. We'd look west into the mellow golden afternoon glow, which would highlight the trunks of elderly pink and grey angaphoras. My spirit sang at the thought.

A path ran along one side of the block. It served as a short cut in the cul-de-sac, through to the local school and a new arcade of shops. In my imagination, I heard children running past. Nearby was a park with playground and oval; all excellent amenities for raising a family and a delightful area in which to grow old.

I asked Thomas many times if I could organise builders' quotes.

He'd say, "We don't know what we want.'

'I thought we did.'

The reluctant one's frown said don't-press-it. Non-decisions around the build taught me to sit back. To build our own home was a dream which our privileged generation could afford, but I needed to move at team pace, to respect my husband's pace, which was very different to mine.

Before marriage, I'd made significant independent decisions: bought cars, land, travelled. I could sleep on decisions but now they passed me by. I said to Thomas, 'Do you realise that when you don't make a decision it means you're actually making a decision?'

He smiled.

I said, 'I can't help but feel that you're delaying the build. Why?'

He chuckled. 'What's the hurry?'

# Snail Mail

It was towards the end of our first year of marriage when I had to take time off work to have an operation. It was a busy time of year: exams, reports and preparations for Open Day but my new GP insisted I be operated on immediately.

'Can I put it off until the school holidays?'

'You're at risk of internal bleeding because you have either a pregnancy in the fallopian tube or a large ovarian cyst.'

After the operation, Sister wheeled me back to the ward from Recovery. She said, 'I've never seen anyone go in looking so grey and come out looking so rosy.'

A few days later, I was allowed to go home provided I convalesce in someone's care. It was decided that Thomas and I would stay with Mum and Dad for a week or two.

The results of the operation were good. The cyst was benign. It had been an active ovarian cyst with quite a history. Pathology showed it was twelve years old and had eaten the right ovary. It was the size of a five-month foetus and had haemorrhaged twice. Looking back, I know exactly when those times were. Even as I write this in the twenty-first century, it still takes years for an accurate diagnosis of endometriosis. Mine took twelve. While it used to be considered a 'woman's issue', today researchers have found it rampaging further afield than the womb. In rare cases, it's been found in men and animals, too.

During my recuperation period, Mum was caring and watchful.

She brought me cups of tea and biscuits and tempting home-made nibblies. Now that the toxins had gone from my body, the priorities were for me to regain weight and build up my strength.

The daybed was folded up each morning. If I needed a rest during the day, I could go inside and lie on my parents' bed. I was resting in there one morning when Mum came in and rummaged in her wardrobe. She seemed to be there for ages.

'Are you okay? What are you looking for?'

'I have something to give you. I think it's safe to give it to you now.'

'That sounds intriguing.'

'It's not.' She rummaged some more. 'It's in here somewhere. It belongs to you. I feel guilty about it but -' Mum pulled out a large official-looking brown envelope and handed it to me. 'Here. I don't know what you're going to do with it.'

In the top left-hand corner it read On Her Majesty's Service, Teachers College, Armidale.

I recognised the handwriting straight away. My gut flipped. My heart crashed gears. A couple of years ago, I'd been waiting to hear from him.

'How come you have it?'

'Well, I didn't give it to you when it first arrived - I thought it'd unsettle you.'

'How long have you had it?'

'When you were in Moss Vale.'

'Mum, that's nearly two years.'

'I've been waiting for the right time.'

'What do you mean?'

Mum deepened her tone. 'Now I don't want any trouble, do you understand? You won't act on it, will you?'

'I don't even know what it is yet but whatever it is, it's a bit late for me to reply. Mum, how could you? Why?'

'Just so long as you know there's no turning back. You're a married woman now. You'll have to get rid of it before your husband gets home.'

'You knew I was waiting to hear from him.'

'You'd just got engaged.'

'Even so.'

'He's divorced. You don't want to get caught up in all that sort of thing.'

I sensed Mum's reasons for interfering and she had a blind spot when it came to Thomas. He was her picture-perfect son-in-law. Then there was the dreaded whispered word - divorce - with 'the other one,' as she referred to Ed.

'But, Mum, after all our talks and you never said a word.'

'I know and I've already said that I felt guilty - you needn't go on about it.' She patted down her apron. 'Do you need anything more to eat?'

I shook my head. I wasn't going to open the envelope until she left the room, although I suspected Mum already knew its contents. I waited. I needed privacy. I owed it respect.

My mother's interference was on a par to taking my life into her hands without asking my permission. I was gobsmacked. She'd interfered in an overly-protective-mother-knows-best way. I felt the power of a tsunami heart rush when I looked at Ed's distinctive handwriting.

I pulled out a manuscript. It was an early version of his book of poems. Inside the first page he'd written, 'Dear Anne, that you may better understand how I think and why I act as I do.'

I'd already read some of his poems when we were together. I knew how much they meant to him. Most were new to me, but some held loving memories which moved me to tears. But, I had to be careful. If Mum came in and found me upset, she'd want to get rid of it, not that I would. He wrote,

*Young loving*
*Arm in arming*
*Good place for hugging,*
*Sunny Sunday Afternooning*
*Sydney Domain...*
*Springtime's thin grace*

*Is a woman I loved...*

These lines brought back memories and I remembered the depth of his gentle love and how deeply I loved him.

It wasn't until some fifty years later, when Ed read my memoir, *Pumpkin*, did he learn about Mum's interference and how she'd hidden his manuscript. In response, he sent me a poem, *Pumpkin Girl*.

*'Having just read your earthquake of a book...*
*long-waves of after-shocks bend to the*
*core of our star-cross-ed-ness...*
*and how I loved the slender girl*
*I took to Manly Beach...'*

It was distressing to learn that Ed had jumped the unreasonably high bar I'd set for him. He and the universe had been on track. The outcome of the hiding of the manuscript reminded me of the Chinese proverb which says that the flapping of a butterfly's wings can be felt on the other side of the world with long-term effects down the years. This simple act sent out ripples which touched lives in a way no-one could foresee.

Mum walked into the bedroom. 'You're not still reading that thing, are you? Your husband won't be very pleased if he finds you... what are you going to do with it?'

'I'll keep it. He's been writing it for years.'

'If you keep it you're asking for trouble.'

'I'll put it in my library. It's special. He might have it published one day.'

And he did, many years later.

'Well, if you want my advice, you'll put it away. The day's getting on and Thomas will be home before you know it.'

My recovery was great thanks to Mum's conscientious care. She made no more references to the snail mail and neither did I. It was too late to undo what had been done. The consequences of Mum's actions were too heavy, overwhelming, so I tucked them away. I was a responsible married woman now.

Thomas and I returned home. There were plenty of jobs to be done. The garden looked neglected. It was an excellent training ground for the day we'd have our own. I'd always had a garden of sorts since I was little. I hoped that soon we'd be in our own home, designing our own garden, but we needed a builder first.

It was a quiet Saturday morning when Thomas went out to mow the lawn. I pottered in the garden nearby. Just as he finished the last of the mowing, Cecil from across the road walked over and spoke to him.

Thomas waved back to me as he walked away with Cecil. I smiled, pleased to see him going, considering Thomas usually avoided neighbours. This was a first.

He returned some time later, unusually chatty. 'I'm so impressed by what they've done. They showed me their newly decorated dining room. It's plush red and gold embossed wallpaper. I'd like to do something like that one day.'

When he flourished his would-be-decorator's hands, there was something different about him. Thomas was already a handsome man but as he stood in the soft southern light in front of the window, he looked quite beautiful. It dismayed me. I didn't know why. A weary weight of woolly sadness settled on my chest.

Thomas stretched back into the armchair in his tight blue short shorts, which revealed light-coloured thighs. He spread his legs and drifted off into a sleepy daze in the middle of the day.

At school, a small group of us liked to sit outside during recess and lunch. We'd carry our tea and coffee out and pull up random spare kindergarten chairs and sit in a circle.

Fee was a super-cool unflappable member of staff but she'd been uncharacterisitically snappy of late.

Someone said, 'Are you okay? Is Baz okay?'

'No.' Fee's voice broke. 'You know our house guest, Nico.'

'The one you adore?'

'Yes, that one,' and we laughed. 'Well, he's Baz's lover.'

Their beautiful house guest, Nico, who'd met Baz six months earlier when Baz had been travelling solo in Italy, had come to Australia and was staying with them.

No one wanted to step on Fee's grief so we sat in silence.

She sighed. 'I found out by accident. I can't believe it. I didn't see it. The boys were away and I had something to get out of the top shelf of the wardrobe. It was in the spare room where Nico slept. I found expensive coffee table books, pulled them down and it was all gay porn - so I put them out on the dining table so when they came home they'd see I'd found them.'

I had no idea what she was talking about - gay porn and men with men? 'What do you mean, they were lovers?'

'They're homosexuals.'

I'd heard the word before but had no idea what it meant. 'What's a homosexual?'

Everyone laughed so much they nearly fell off their colourful kindergarten chairs. At least, I made Fee laugh. But we had to be careful. A whiff of this mustn't creep into the main staffroom. Any hint of gossip around a member of staff could mean instant dismissal.

Fee said, 'A homosexual is a man who's attracted to another man.'

'Really?'

'Baz is a closet one. He kept it a secret.'

Then we talked about lesbians. It seemed appropriate that I was sitting on a kindergarten chair while learning the ABC's of sexual behaviours, of which, up until now, I'd been oblivious.

Fee said, 'Baz admitted they were lovers straight away - they moved out last weekend.'

While the rest of the group continued to listen to Fee's situation, I struggled to untangle a naive belief that, once married, you sorted out your problems and there'd never be a reason for you to break your vows, ever. I have to say that Fee's disclosure during morning recess shifted the foundations of my double-brick house of beliefs. I could see her situation was untenable. How sad! It was so unfair! Baz shouldn't have married her. While he might've suffered keeping it quiet, because in those days it was still a crime, a secret, but for Fee it was devastating.

I sat there in the sunshine on that pivotal morning in the midst of a rich fellowship of women. Love in action. I watched how they supported Fee gently and without judgement. It was sobering and I felt privileged to be there.

That afternoon, I drove home thinking about parts of my own life: school, friends, family, our block of land - all good but the personal side - the intimate companionship side of our marriage - well - it wasn't what I'd expected at all.

Fee's situation niggled. I wished I could stop thinking about it but I couldn't. After dinner, I said to Thomas, 'I have to tell you about Fee. It's so sad.'

'Mmm?'

'I learnt today what a homosexual is. It turns out that Baz is a homosexual, a closet one.'

'Oh.'

'Can you believe it?'

'It wouldn't surprise me.'

'Why?'

Thomas pulled a face. Shuffled his feet. 'I never liked him - made my skin crawl.'

'Really? I don't mind him. He's a very good host. I can't imagine what it's like for Fee now. I wonder how you'd know if someone's a closet homosexual? But you wouldn't, would you? I suppose that's the whole point.'

'There's two across the road.'

'What do you mean?'

'Donald and Cecil. They're - you know,' Thomas said with a laugh. 'I call them the Odd Couple.'

'They seem normal.'

'I don't know how they get away with it.'

'With what?'

'Living like that. It's a crime. I'm surprised no one's reported them.'

'Being a homosexual is a crime? Why?'

'It just is.'

I said, 'Obviously they're not closet ones. I can't stop thinking about Fee. They've been married ten years and to think it's all been a lie. She's been a cover.'

'I wouldn't worry. They live a good life. They've got lots of friends.'

'Yes, one too many, I'd say.'

I tried to imagine how a man could have sex with another man but didn't ask. What else did Thomas know about our neighbours? I felt secretly proud of Donald and Cecil if what Thomas said was true. They had to be brave to live in the open like that.

Donald and Cecil lived in a neat white weatherboard with a lush front garden; the avenue's show piece. On Saturday mornings, C & D tended their front gardens topless. Strong arms dug up garden beds. Shaven sweaty mahogany chests glowed in the morning sun. Their skimpy shorts revealed well-toned thighs and muscular calves. As far as I could see, there was nothing to obsess about, but Thomas liked watching them. He'd pace in front of the large room window and mumble.

I used to say, 'You'd better come away from the window. They might think you're staring.'

The middle-aged men were well-liked in the small community. During the working week, they left each morning to catch a bus to the city around the same time we left. They were both straight-backed and well dressed and carried briefcases, just like Thomas.

The neighbours on our western side had been a nun and priest. They'd left the church, married and had two lively children. The couple on our eastern side were partners, a blended family, an increasing trend. Their teenage and adult children came and went with the tide.

One afternoon, Thomas came home from work and dropped his briefcase by the hallstand and said, 'I have to go to Newcastle for three weeks.'

'Newcastle? Why?'

'Kevin said it'll be good experience.'

Kevin was an older mentor of Thomas's, in the predominantly Protestant-based Public Service. Outside of work, they were volunteer editor and subeditor of a high-quality monthly nationwide magazine for a railway historical society.

I was unaware that Thomas could transfer out of Sydney. I was surprised when he came home after three weeks up north with the news,

'The job's mine if I want it. It has to be advertised first but now that I've spent three weeks there, I'm first in line. I meet all criteria.'

'For how long?'

'Two years.'

'Two years. Do you want to go?'

'Do you think I should? Kevin said it's a good career move.'

'I suppose it'd be an adventure - but what would we do with the build?'

'Delay it.'

'Will we definitely come back after two years?'

'Yes.'

I was excited for Thomas but there was a problem. My work. Only weeks earlier I'd been asked by the mistress-in-charge if I'd be interested in training as deputy. Training would commence towards the end of the year. The current deputy planned to retire in eighteen months' time.

'There's my work and I've already agreed to training.'

'It's only for two years.'

Kevin, his boss, and his wife, Pru, invited us to dinner. By dessert, it was agreed that the transfer was a wonderful opportunity for Thomas.

Kevin said, 'It's an excellent promotion and it'll put you in line for higher grades more quickly.'

Who was I to stop him?

The next morning, I had a meeting with the Mistress-in-Charge. I told her about Thomas's transfer and how it would impact.

She made a sensible suggestion. 'If it's only for two years, perhaps your husband could commute and come home on weekends.'

I hadn't thought of that and it made sense. It meant building could proceed and, later in the year, I could start my training.

That afternoon after work, I called in to see Mum to tell her the news. I floated Miss P's idea.

Without hesitation, she said, 'You can't do that. You're his wife. It's your place to be by his side.'

Miss P's suggestion was ahead of its time and she was in a different position to me. Her first loyalty was to the school, whereas mine was to my husband. It was 1972. In our circle, a woman didn't have a career. She had jobs which were expected to be given up when we fell pregnant with our first child. From then on, it was our duty to support our husband's career and wishes.

Women, like me, who'd gone onto further education, who were part of the change in the air, were caught up in the rapid change of the 60's and 70's which didn't fit with our mothers' or grandmothers' expectations.

It was difficult for us to make a stand because there was no proof yet to show that the sky wouldn't fall in, and the Empire wouldn't crumble if, for example, I stayed in Sydney and Thomas commuted to and from Newcastle on a weekly basis.

I came around to the belief that a two-year transfer wouldn't be such a sacrifice if it helped Thomas in the long term. He'd been unsettled and appeared to be excited about the move. The deputy head mentioned that perhaps she could delay her retirement for another two years.

# Gaytime Caravan Park

1972. Newcastle. I went to pick up Thomas after work. It was supposed to be peak hour but in this small city, so unlike Sydney, I could park wherever I liked. I parked under an old plane tree, right out the front of the office's modest front entrance. Another car had parked in a similar fashion, further along, almost too close to the corner. Golden leaves skittered along the gutter in the breeze. The autumn chill encroached on the late afternoon.

Thomas appeared. He jumped down the few front steps of the office and headed towards the car. He came around to the driver's side. I was expected to slide across to the passenger seat while he dropped his briefcase in the back. After he hopped into the driver's seat, he leant across and kissed me on the cheek, smelling of pen and paper and of that stale odour of three men cooped up in a small room, all day, organising other people's lives.

When he pulled out from the kerb, I expected we'd turn left but he went straight ahead.

'Oh, I thought -' then I stopped.

Early on in our marriage, Thomas had let it be known by some well-placed sighs that questions annoyed him. At times, I felt like that pesky kid who was meant to be seen and not heard. In this instance, it seemed only fair that I know where I was going. After all, we were driving into our future.

'Oh, I thought we'd go that way. Where are we going?'

'To buy sheets. They don't supply them.'

'We've got plenty of sheets. I packed some. Look.' I pointed towards the back of the car filled with linen and clothes but my words fell into a pit. I heard them drop. I heard that sound increasingly these days. My role seemed to be that of silent partner. Thomas's answers to questions were either opaque or non-existent.

I'd reproach myself - stand up for yourself- you have every right to know what's going on - it's your life, too. Thomas's increasingly restricted style of communication unnerved me. I'd assumed we'd make decisions together. Before we moved up, we'd made a decision to stay in the motel until we leased a unit, but since I'd arrived, I found myself in 24/7 catch-up. Apparently, arrangements had changed.

Thomas turned right into the narrow busy street. My diminishing self clung onto the car door handle. 'What are we looking for?'

'A shop. They say it's cheap.'

The car inched forward. Thankfully there was a parking spot. I willed Thomas to park quickly but to no avail. He took his time and traffic built up behind us while he parked the car, perfectly parallel to the gutter.

We walked into a new fandangled discount store with lots of ultra bright lights and deafening bouncy music. I walked down the first jam-packed overstocked aisle dodging bargain hunters and in-your-face low-price labels.

Thomas called out and held up packages. I waved and stopped looking for the double bed sheets I believed we didn't need. I met him at the checkout.

We drove a long way out of town into dusk.

'Where is it?'

'Not far.'

At one point, we stopped at a set of red lights. As I stared into the murky dusk I was shocked when I realised I was looking straight into the back of a large truck. I goosebumped and rearranged my unsettled self. I shivered. This was it. This was the nightmare I'd had when I first started going out with Thomas.

*The nightmare - the black back of the truck directly in front of me.*

*It's moving too slow and we're speeding towards its - blackness on the freeway. In the dream, we almost crash into terrifying blackness. I try to wake out of the dream but am paralysed. I realise it's only a dream. Tell myself I have to rewind and avoid the crash. In dreamland, I consciously rewind the action to the time before the threat of a crash. This time, I move the truck into the next lane and overtake it. I wake gasping.*

It was a relief when Thomas finally turned left, away from the truck. My stomach flipped. I'd said nothing to him about the earlier nightmare. We didn't talk about things like that. Instead, I'd shared it with my unconditional companion, my journal. I'd wondered at the time what the vivid nightmare meant. Being influenced by Jung, I recorded it in my journal but had no idea of its meaning.

We pulled up outside the front gate of Gaytime Caravan Park. Six o'clock on the dot. The entrance gate was already closed. I fully understood its reluctance to let us in. I even heard the gate whisper. Well, if it wasn't the gate whispering, it was my gut. I had to resist the urgent whispers to run, run now.

The park attendant poked his head out of the small office window and yelled; not quite the greeting I'd expected. We entered to all appearances as a couple but one of us definitely didn't want to be there. I caught my breath and pressed myself back on the seat. I tried to breathe easy. Whatever was coming didn't feel good.

Gaytime was on the southern edge of town, somewhere south of the city, nowhere near Thomas's work. We drove into the park through elongated shadows until we reached the last row alongside the busy Pacific Highway.

Vision was poor in the dim moments before the automatic street and park lights came on. We reached the van in the duskiest part of dusk where putting a hand out needed light to see form. I continued to fight off panic and suppressed an urge to cry. I scolded myself - don't be silly - this is an adventure although it didn't feel like one. What were we doing in this particular caravan park? I couldn't believe I'd agreed to it. Actually, I hadn't.

Thomas's plans proved to be consistently impractical and I was expected to be grateful. I didn't want to share toilets and showers in peak hour with workers and tourists in the amenities. My shoulders carried a ridiculously heavy yoke of dread as I stood outside the van and watched Thomas, the man-who-organised-the-van, climb in and inspect. He poked his head out and smiled. It met with his approval; a priority these days.

I stepped inside and saw two sets of double bunks. The double bed's potential fitted in under a collapsible breakfast table. Only one of us would fit on it comfortably.

I said, 'They've given us the wrong van.'

Thomas smiled. He turned and pulled out two packets of sheets, the ones he'd bought at the cheap shop. He opened the packets with a flourish. They were single-bed pink and blue flannelette sheets.

He shook out each sheet. 'Pink for you and blue for me,' and laughed. He fitted them onto the lower bunks.

When he'd finished, he turned and waited for me to thank him but I was too distracted by the flapping of the elephant's ears.

I didn't want to see what the elephant saw, but I couldn't unsee it. I had an urge to pick up the car keys and pretend I was popping out to buy dinner. When out of sight, I'd turn left instead of right onto the highway. I wouldn't go to the shops. I'd head straight down the highway to I don't know where, to I don't know who, to anywhere but here.

'How did you know to buy single sheets?'

'This was the only van left'.

'We could've stayed at the motel.'

'We couldn't afford it.'

'Yes, we could.'

A futile discussion now. The deed was done. I didn't know what to do next. The single beds screamed at me. I couldn't bear to look at them or at Thomas.

The vibe in the caravan was every bit as tense and as drained as I felt. I busied myself picking up Thomas's needs and laundering his moods. I'd hoped to cook something simple for tea but we had no matches. Apparently, I should've known to buy them. I was tempted to ask Thomas if I could use his recent surge of exasperation to light the gas.

I could've combusted and probably should've. This was a God-awful situation. I distracted myself by unpacking this and that and tried to hide from myself a struggle with a truth I didn't want to see.

'We need a bigger van, Thomas, one with a proper double bed.'

'There's nothing wrong with this one. We won't be here long.'

In my spare time, and while Thomas was at work, Thomas had told me I was responsible for shopping and meals. He reminded me that the laundry was at the other end of the park behind the amenities block. The washing lines were behind that. I had the choice of ironing approximately ten white shirts a week for Thomas either on the kitchen table or in some far flung laundry.

After a couple of days, I said, 'Thomas we need a better van for the time we're here.'

'I suppose so.'

'I'll organise it if you're happy with that.'

'I suppose it'd be good to have one not so close to the road.'

'Can we look for a unit? We hardly have any room.' I disliked clutter and I'd lost the battle to keep the van in order. I had a solution. 'Let's carry stuff in baskets on our head.'

There was no witty retort. I'd hoped that humour would be a constant staple in our diet but with the move north we walked through a portal into a hungry humourless dimension where Thomas lost his wit and I lost my appetite and vertigo revisited. Bouts of cystitis screamed, 'I'm so pissed off.'

An onlooker would've seen us as husband and wife sitting outside the van on our holiday makers' chairs. No raised voices. The husband read his magazines and would occasionally look up and scour his surroundings. The wife read a book and often looked up and spoke to her husband.

I was the onlooker. I'd never given any thought to the intricacies of coupledom until now. In my unsettled state, I began to scrutinise us and the actions of couples. Some comforted and touched each other readily. Some leaned into each other as they spoke. There was eye contact and comforting smiles. This wasn't us.

One night as we sat and ate dinner, Thomas said, 'Let's sell both blocks of land.'

'Why?'

The Sydney block was my financial responsibility and we lived off Thomas's salary. The other block, my beloved mountain block, I'd purchased years earlier. It was already paid off.

'Roy says we can buy house and land here for the same price as a block of land in Sydney.'

'That's true, but you can't compare the two.'

'There's only one area up here that I like. I've always liked the look of it from the train.'

'But if we sold our land, it'd be difficult buying back at Sydney's prices. We were lucky getting that block. I thought we were going to rent up here.'

'Roy said he came up from Sydney and he's never looked back. He wouldn't want to live anywhere else.'

'That's Roy. Not us. Let's rent a unit first and get to know the area. We can afford the rent.'

The idea of selling our land was a shock.

Thomas said, 'You think too deeply, sweetheart. The way you go about things-'

His line sounded familiar. I'd heard it so often from my mother. 'You think too deeply.'

Maybe they were right. The constant clipping of my wings had the desired effect. I soon became my husband's secretary, under his direction. His instructions were for me to finalise the move out of the rental property, organise the sale of the Sydney block. I'd said no to selling the mountain block. I was to undertake house-hunting and in my spare time cook, wash, iron, tidy, clean, shop and get a job.

Amazingly, I found occasional moments of quiet. It was usually at the end of day. Within that stillness, I sensed the formation of a dramatic curve. I could almost reach out and touch it. I couldn't tell yet if it was a tragic or comic curve.

When I woke of a morning, every cell in my body and gut protested but I'd remind myself that, sometime in the future, I'd look back on this time as a wise investment for the family's future. With this creep of disorientation, it felt like I'd escaped up into the left-hand corner of a Chagall. I had to get down; ground myself; remind myself that I was of stoic stock. I'd steal myself in this steel city.

# The Class Warrior

It was the last week of the May school holidays. We'd just settled into the caravan when one of my husband's colleagues, whose nephew was the Director of Catholic Education in the Hunter Region, gave my husband his number and said for me to ring. He'd spoken to his nephew and told him I was looking for a job.

I was reluctant to ring straight away. I needed at least a fortnight to do all the admin things that needed to be done but, at the same time, I was grateful for the introduction so rang for an interview. After the phone call and interview, I started work the following week, first week of second term.

Thomas's directions on how to find the school were unique. 'Drive west and look out for the old church on top of the hill. That's where the school is – right behind it.'

The old church stood like a beacon once I found the right road. I parked at the back of the school and walked up to the playground. To the west of the church was an L shaped line of portables situated behind the beacon. There was also a stand alone building to its right which served as a school assembly and church meeting hall. In front of it was a swathe of steep overgrown grass, unsafe for ball games or regular play of any kind. The main playground had accident-prone potholes in the asphalt. The overall impression of the portables was grime grey on grey grime. I'm sure it wasn't but that was my impression.

Introductions to staff took place on the veranda of the main portable. We gathered outside the principal's office. Being situated on the top of a hill, the wind whipped us into a tight huddle and slapped our calves.

I could see Head Sister standing in her office staring at me. The office was hardly big enough for a small desk and chair on either side. Sister stood as still as the tall grey metal filing cabinet she stood beside, opposite the open door. The rest of the room looked as bare as Mother Hubbard's cupboard. It looked as though it was waiting for someone to move in.

Deputy Sister M introduced me to the staff. Sister M was a warm motherly type, short and plump, full of light, the type I could easily have greeted with a hug. Head Sister finally made her entrance by swishing her black habit as she strode out of the office. She eyed me up and down as if I had something to hide.

I smiled trying to cover a childlike urge to empty my pockets and show her I wasn't hiding anything but I didn't have any pockets. After the introductions, I was shown a small room. It was the staffroom about the size of a postage stamp. Now I knew why announcements were given on the veranda.

Soon I was taken to the third grade classroom. The classroom was threadbare and had an ugly-in-your-face toughness. It exuded a take-us-or-leave-us attitude; an example of unnecessary poverty of spirit. Not every classroom looked as neglected as this one.

I stood in the midst of culture shock when the first morning bell clanged.

Head Sister introduced me to the class and instructed me, in front of my students, to send them to her if they misbehaved. 'I have the cane and they know I'll use it.'

I'd never been in a school which used the cane, nor had I been told to send students to the office for discipline. I hadn't dealt with clan wars before either. Battles raged, punches were thrown, lips split.

'P, sit down! B, sit!'

P cried because B had whacked him on the back of the head with the sharp edge of a ruler. Their friends, loyal followers, cheered and whooped. Multiply this scene by one hundred and it'd still be an understatement of the infighting which dominated the introduction to each school day. Gentle spirits knew how to blend into the background. I wanted to blend with them but had to remind myself that I was the teacher. I quickly learnt that many of these children were related and carried heavy historical family baggage on tender young shoulders. They fought as if their family's name depended on it.

About six weeks into teaching third grade, I made an appointment at a recommended GP's practice. When I sat in Dr F's surgery, I noticed first of all a hardy camellia outside the window. I didn't know it then, but I'd come back and sit in this same chair over the next few years and draw strength from that camellia.

I watched it survive in the wrong location: it budded, bloomed and continued to boast dark green leaves. To be at its best, the camellia needed a degree of protection and afternoon shade but it stood in front of the north facing window in all weathers with no protection other than its own will to survive. Many a camellia would've faded but not this one.

I needed to talk to Dr. F about my increasing nervousness. It didn't seem to matter where I went in this city, I felt ill at ease. I experienced waves of anxiety and nausea in the mornings shortly after I arrived at school. The inner trembling started around ten o'clock. The school situation held some new shock every day, and living with Thomas had become more and more unpredictable.

The fresh-faced, friendly Scot prescribed a low dose of Valium, a popular new drug for anxiety. I took it and the shakes and nausea subsided. It took the edge off the day but to the extent that my edges blurred. The flatness and dullness of each day was worse than anxiety. It was so depressing.

After a couple of months, I decided to stop taking it but it was difficult. I shook worse than before so I came up with a plan. I increased my cups of sweetened hot Milo and cut the tablets back gradually. The warm sugared milk became my comfort zone and I successfully stopped taking the mind-numbing tablets. I gave myself pep talks instead, the first being, 'Don't be such a wuss'.

Over the ensuing weeks, I began to enjoy the company of the friendly staff. We shared and laughed.

One of them, Val, an avowed humanist, who used to teach in very rough schools in Britain, laughed when I expressed my shock at the neglect of the playground and wondered how to stop the constant clan wars. She said, 'This is nothing.'

To watch her accept what should've been better and to see how she worked around the obstacles eventually became an inspiration. I invented diversions for my class, a class which held within it rage and hopelessness.

There was moderate success and Head Sister was curious. 'You haven't sent anyone to me.'

I prided myself that I'd never have any need to send a child to the principal. After all, they were my class, my responsibility.

'Some of them are a handful,' I said, 'but mostly they're fine.'

But, one morning, a wiry young boy tripped his cousin then fell on him. His cousin lay splattered in the aisle and couldn't move. I feared he was badly hurt. With some help from the children, we got him up and helped him back to his seat. There was no sickbay or office to send Billy to, apart from Head Sister.

I turned to him and said, 'Right, that's it, up to Sister. Now.'

Everyone kept their heads down until he strode back into the class, full-chested. He was eight years old and had the swagger of a rugged old man in heavy work boots.

Someone whispered to him,' How many?'

'Six.'
'He got six.'
'Wow!'
'He got six.'
'Choice.'

I realised Billy had walked back into the classroom a hero. Who'd have thought that the cane was medal material? Not me, so the biggest improvement in behaviour management happened by chance.

These cousins were firecrackers but the class warrior had the shorter fuse so it wasn't long before he assaulted his cousin again.

'Send him to Sister, Miss, send him to Sister.'

There was no way I'd send anyone to Sister ever again and have the tough guy status raised.

'Come here, please.'

'Didn't do nothin'.'

'You did and I want you to say sorry then go and stand up the back and look at the colour of the wall. Don't turn around, just look at the colour of the wall and think about why you're standing there. When you're ready, come and tell me.'

'Send me to sister, Miss. It's better going to Sister.'

'You're not going.'

'Give him the ruler, Miss.'

'No, I want him to think about what happened.'

Heads turned as they watched the class warrior face the wall. For all appearances, the usual culprits looked as though they'd settled but they hadn't. The class was on high alert. Soon there were whispers.

'He's crying. Billy's crying.'

They looked at me. Obviously, it was my fault. Did I know that the class warrior would cry? Did he know he could cry?

I walked up to him and said he was to stand there for another five minutes. That'd give him time to compose himself and I said, 'When you're ready come and tell me why you've been standing here.'

Five minutes later, Billy stood beside me and said for all to hear, 'Sorry, Miss.'

Class whispered, 'He said sorry. Billy said sorry'

'And?'

'I'm not allowed to punch.'

'That's right and why not?'

Very soon the warrior took his place at his desk, put his head down and worked. He was the stereotypical underachiever. Thanks to him, the class was never the same. When they came into class with some tiff, I'd remind them where they were and how they were to treat each other.

I didn't let on that I was learning as much from them as they were from me. I was on a sharp learning curve both at school and at home and in this new town. Every which way was so different to anything I'd ever experienced.

I needed to introduce the students to moments of beauty in their classroom. I started by introducing flowers. I put a fresh vase of flowers on my desk every Monday morning. I'd hold a flower or fern up and talk about its name and we'd count the petals and stamens and wonder why they needed them.

I shared with them how I'd had a small garden at their age. I drew on the board a glimpse of how it looked - the alternate-coloured small rocks which I'd painted with leftover black and yellow indoor paint which my father used to paint the kitchen. I drew an idea of the plaster of paris moulds of rabbit, lion and one of the seven dwarves I used to make and paint to decorate my garden.

Very soon we were looking for spare vases for the flowers brought in by students any day of the week. They'd share with the class whatever they wanted to say about them; where they came from; why they picked them. They began to share family stories. The flowers brought in local news and current affairs which became an important part of the day.

The back noticeboard filled with their drawings, pictures and photos.

We began regular art lessons and they hung their paintings around the room. Art classes were unheard of for this class, who'd unfortunately had an incredibly disruptive year. I was their third teacher. It was said the two other teachers, one a nun and the other a lay teacher, had both gone off on stress leave. All I could glean from a clammed-up staff was that it had something to do with Head Sister.

This struggling working-class area, made up of long-standing families, had a lot of inbreeding. Children were first or second cousins. There seemed to be few opportunities for these lively imaginative students outside of school but one privilege for them in school was Kodaly, which ran until funding finished. I'd never seen it at work in a classroom so I sat in on lessons given by an instructor who visited each class teaching the Kodaly method once a week. I noticed that after the lesson there was a ribbon of peace and smiles and unexpected courtesies all round.

The good news was that when the short course finished, the school acquired the instruments. There were no bookings for them first thing in the morning so, once or twice a week, during maths time, we had musical maths. We'd sit on the floor in a big circle and work together, plaiting Daa-dada-daa-daa, daa-dada-daa-daa...' breathing and clapping, singing and clapping; a universal language: togetherness, connection, communication.

Billy became a productive, helpful member of the class with obvious leadership skills. While he still had the occasional disruptive day out on the playground, in the classroom he shone with purpose and self belief and this class warrior kept surprising himself, and his loyal disciples who strived to keep up with him.

# First Home

We put our Belrose block on the market and I prayed it wouldn't sell. It sold immediately. No longer could I dream about our children playing in the backyard or running down to the park to play on the swings. I could no longer imagine sitting out the back on a summer's evening chatting and raving about the fading light and pointing out the brilliant washes of violet, pink and gold in the sunset.

When the block sold, Thomas said, 'That's good because we'll be up here longer.'

'How much longer?'

'It could be three or four years. There's another promotion coming up.'

I didn't want to hear that.

After work, I drove around Newcastle getting a sense of place and looking for either land or a house to buy. Some areas lacked clean air. There were very few tree-lined streets. I looked for swathes of freshly mowed lawns and lush gardens, shaded by tall spreading trees, but couldn't find any. An occasional new development ushered in some green but most streets were steeped in their particular history, so different to a few kilometres down the road.

I followed maps; hunted down ads. I found a promising bushy block of land for sale on the high side of the road in a new development. We put on a holding deposit, found a house plan and I started to dream again, but Thomas's boss, Roy, said to Thomas, 'Buy an established home. That way you can move in straight away.'

Thomas took back the holding deposit and I started to search again, this time looking for a house. I discovered a suburb in a seemingly good location. It was a little further out than we'd discussed. I walked along its main street and peered into real estate windows. Houses were remarkably cheap. It seemed to be a quiet pleasant location with a protective hill, and a creek which seemed perfect for canoeing, and it was situated close to an adventurous waterway.

A local real estate agent took me to see a new house on the high side of a steep street. The house was everything we needed but as I walked along the front path my feet felt heavy and the street had a noticeably barren look.

I said, 'No-one has a garden. There are no plants or trees.'

At no stage did the agent mention the controversial lead smelter nearby. He had a job to do, a pay cheque to collect and a commission to look forward to; a commission laced with toxins.

'You can head up that way a few streets along.' He pointed south. 'Might be more what you're looking for.'

I was puzzled as to why I felt so physically weighed down. After some research about the lead smelter, I found that the area had once been an oasis and was now a potential graveyard. Everyone who lived and worked there walked in lead boots. Uninformed families were the unwitting victims. Years later I read, 'Lead has a half-life of at least seven hundred years.'

The smelter closed in 2003 but I'm shocked to read that today, in 2025, there are new developments, including the building of a new school.

I went to another estate agent. 'We'd like north at the back, three bedrooms and...'

The agent took me to see homes set on busy street corners and on steep slopes facing west. Back in the office, I asked if he had anything else on the books.

'I might but next time bring your husband.'

'He can't be here because he's at work.'

'He's the one who decides.'

'Not really. The idea is I find something we both might like then he'll come and look at them.'

The pointed-shoe-one tidied his already tidy desk. 'It's a waste of time showing you without him.'

A teaching colleague suggested a particular agency. 'It's where transfers go. You don't need your husband.'

I sat with one of their agents. He pulled out a large notepad. 'Now, what is it we're looking for?' and there was a rush of fresh air.

'Preferably north facing at the back, quiet street, three bedrooms, a bus route to town.'

The bright-faced, friendly one looked into his file and drew out five cards. 'Right,' he said, 'let's go.'

He'd listened and I could've bought every one of the properties.

Back in the office, he said, 'Do a drive-by with hubby and get back to me.'

The drive-by determined it. There was no doubt which location Thomas preferred. It met all his criteria. It was a carbon copy of his nearby train friends' homes and his boss's, all within close proximity.

It wouldn't have been my first or second choice. Living on the low side of a street and not on a ridge, and living in a house snuggled into a small valley with no access to southerly summer breezes, was not my ideal location but I consoled myself. It was only for two years. Well, maybe a year or two more.

While the locals believed that their town was a well kept secret, and tried to keep it to themselves, outsiders, more commonly southern city slickers like us, were treated as outlaws. So there was the sense of being an emigrant and there was an unsettling vibe that bad news was always just around the corner. On the local evening news, there'd be some horrible event like a murder or a dramatic suburban suicide just over the hill. I didn't realise the world was so small. I'd soon learn that this city was a microcosm, a nationwide representation, well-used for research because of its size, diversity and accessibility.

We bought into a typical nuclear-family neighbourhood. When we bought 7 Elvidge Crescent, there were plans before the council for a proposed estate out the back. It was behind our back fence where glorious tall elderly gums sheltered bellbirds, rosellas and lorikeets. I'd learnt about the development when making inquiries at the council about the area before we bought it. The clerk assured me the proposal probably wouldn't go ahead for at least another twenty or thirty years. We'd be back in Sydney by then.

We bought the well-presented triple-fronted white weatherboard with blue tiles and landscaped frontyard and oversized backyard with beautiful bush behind.

Thomas was even happier when he came home one afternoon and said he'd soon get another promotion. 'Not in Sydney, It's up here. I'd be silly not to take it.'

My heart sank. 'Of course.'

I rang my past employer with the news. 'I'm sorry but it looks like I won't be back for some time. My husband's got another promotion up here - thank you so much for the opportunity.'

'I wish you well, dear. Remember, there's always a place here for you.'

My ties to home were undone one by one. We settled into a hollow, close-hugging valley in a suburban street with selvidged kerbs and hem-lined houses.

One afternoon after work, I drove down our steep driveway and heard bulldozers. I couldn't believe what I saw. Within a few hours, grand eucalypts out the back had gone. I raced up and stood on our back veranda to get a better view. I looked due north to a newly barren stretch of land beyond our boundary. The bleeding gums lay dispossessed. Without dignity. Displaced elderly. Their compliance was frightening.

I stood on the back porch and cried. Rang Thomas. 'You've got no idea what they've done. It's terrible, terrible.'

Within weeks, bird calls were replaced with the din of assault and battery on the flora and fauna on ancient Awabakal land. The resulting progress was unrelenting and without remorse.

Over ensuing months, there was the manifestation of Malverna Robert's folk song, *Little Boxes*. It reminded me of what she wrote in the 1960s when she and her husband were on a road trip. The story goes that they were driving along when Malverna saw a new development. She asked her husband to take the steering wheel so she could write down the words which were coming fast and strong. They still echo today, all about little boxes on a hillside, all looking just the same.

As we sat on our sunny north-facing back veranda, there was the obvious loss of trees and the sprouting of more and more boxes. Yet in spite of the brick jungle mushrooming out the back, stars shone brighter at night than any pompous display of designer porch lights.

At our end of the crescent, on our side of the street, the low side, young marrieds reared two, three, four children. We literally looked up to those who lived on the high side in older well-established larger, brick homes. Their offspring had reached study/work stage.

When Thomas first transferred, he was told by his workmates, 'Before you do or say anything, remember that up here everyone's somebody's aunt, uncle or cousin three times removed,' and, 'don't buy anything without asking first. There's always someone who knows someone who can give you a good deal.'

And so it was.

After we moved into our house, Val lent us a card table and chairs until I organised the delivery of our second-hand dining table and chairs, sideboard and hallstand bought from my friend's parents. We splurged a couple of pay packets on a beautifully crafted hardwood two seater lounge suite with two swivel rocking arm chairs. The suite took pride of place in our toy-free living room where vases upheld sacrificial offerings to the fertility gods. Blooms turned to the light praying.

'Please, I beg you. Please.'

Our home had a cozy feeling at night when the tall cedar standard lamp lit up the living room. I used to imagine family and friends sitting there chatting and laughing, so I was delighted when one wet afternoon unexpected visitors knocked on the front door.

They were good friends on holidays travelling north. My friend admired our new rather expensive two-seater lounge suite. I knew she'd like it. We had similar tastes.

"But you see,' she said, patting the arm of the brocaded armchair as if a baby's bottom, 'I'd rather have Them than a beautiful lounge.'

# Mould

Elvidge Crescent was our first home. Out the front were three terraces of garden filled with healthy looking roses, strawberries, alyssum; flowers of all kinds. There was a velvet swathe of blue couch and bent lawn. It looked like a bowling green. Down by the fishpond, snuggled into the triple-fronted corners, the one near the front veranda, fuchsias and ferns flourished. Goldfish swam in and around and hid beneath water lilies.

We had a lot to learn about looking after our own home, especially how to handle problems caused by living on a slope on the low side of the street. The garage was down the back under the house next to the laundry. We'd drive down a long steep drive then we'd take a sharp right hand turn at the bottom, on the large concrete apron and keep turning.

We soon discovered that when it rained heavily, water seeped through the garage. Thomas had drawn rough plans for a model railway on three walls in a similar way to Charlie's but the garage had to be dry first. In its darkest corner, old magazines were stacked between the outside wall and a chest of drawers where mould decomposed whatever it could.

It was school holidays and my project was to complete the unpacking and try and air the garage. Thomas had stored things there before we knew about the water problem. Many of my books were still missing so I decided it was time to see if I could find them. At the same time, I could try and rid the garage of all mould.

I expected that everything stored in the corner where the water had seeped through would be too damp and damaged to rescue. Hopefully, none of my books were in any of those piles. I'd been assured they were in the unpacked boxes in the third bedroom.

Wearing gardening gloves, I sprayed the whole area for cockroaches, spiders and fleas. As expected, some things had stuck together and some had disintegrated. They were thrown into the garbage bin.

About halfway down, I found a brown paper bag in surprisingly good condition. I picked it up, walked over into the light and pulled out a magazine. As I flicked through the pages, I saw naked men with other naked men and an array of erect and flacid penises. As I hadn't been a surveyor of these particular body parts, I would never have dreamt such contortions were possible. My heart raced at the sight. This could be devastatingly significant. While part of me didn't want to know, I suspected the owner of the magazine didn't want me to know either.

The full sun beamed in through the front of the garage. My inner world tilted instantly but everything outside looked exactly the same. I looked at the innocent beauty of the Rose garden by the side fence: Peace, Double Delight and Queen Elizabeth all held up their heads, nonplussed. I had no idea what to do. There had to be a next step on this fractured but particularly beautiful powder blue day.

First things first. Don't jump to conclusions. Maybe this magazine doesn't belong to Thomas. There could be an innocent explanation.

I walked back into the garage and dealt with the remains of the damp mouldy pile, which was where I found some of my missing books: the leather covered set of Shakespeare's plays and the *Time Life Nature and Science* series. Mould was thicker the closer to the floor.

I rescued my books and wiped them down all the while apologising to them. I also came across my teaching resources. I spread them out on the drive and wiped down anything I could save and the rest went into the incinerator.

The magazine I'd uncovered was in perfect condition. What to do? I thought of my colleague, Fee, who'd found gay porn. She'd laid it out on the table and waited for a reaction. But what worried me the most was what did it mean for our relationship? Should I throw it away or should I ask Thomas? Would it cause a flare-up or was it mere curiosity on his part?

When Thomas arrived home from work, he dropped his briefcase by the table and poured himself a glass of water. He was sweating from his short walk from the bus stop. After he settled into his recliner, I'd decided there could be no right time.

I asked him about his day, then told him about mine. 'I cleaned out the mouldy part of the garage today and found my books and, oh, this.' I handed him the magazine. 'What does it mean?'

'Oh, that. Someone at work gave it to me.' He stood up, picked up his briefcase, opened it with a flourish and threw in the offending magazine. 'I'll give it back to him if that'll make you happy. It was just something he-' Thomas slammed the briefcase shut, dropped it to the floor and disappeared down the backstairs.

I picked up the briefcase and stood it beside the recliner where it usually sat. I moved across to the kitchen sink, filled a couple of saucepans with water and veggies and put the lamb chops into the vertical griller. If I could keep on keeping on, there'd be a better time to sit down with Thomas when we could talk, without any blame or shame. He was probably shocked like I'd been shocked when I found it. Nothing more was said that night. We ate dinner, watched TV, went to bed.

The next morning was the dawn of a beautiful sunny suburban Saturday. Edge cutters and lawnmowers and children squealed, dogs barked, birds called. After breakfast, Thomas headed downstairs. I assumed he'd mow the lawn.

Since the brown paper bag incident, I'd been treated like I'd been a naughty girl. I cleared the kitchen table and sat in line with the morning sun as it shone through the northern window. I'd catch up on some marking. I expected to hear the edge-cutter's roar in the background but something was different. I walked out onto the back patio and heard what I thought was the car's engine. Where was Thomas going?

I glanced down and saw that the garage door appeared to be closed. I instinctively flew downstairs. Fortunately, the garage wasn't locked. I lifted up the heavy wooden door. The car purred. That's when I saw a rag stuffed into the muffler.

'Thomas, Thomas!'

I raced to the driver's door and opened it. As I did, I registered that the car door's window was partly open. Thomas's head had slumped onto his chest. I reached in, turned off the ignition, all the while calling 'Thomas, Thomas, wake up, wake up.'

I tried to hold up his head, but it was too heavy. I tried to open his eyes. I slapped his cheek. He winced. Good. He was alive. His head dropped back sharply onto the headrest and his mouth gaped wide. I shook so much it was hard taking his pulse. It was regular. Phew! What on earth? Why on earth?

The fright, the relief, the confusion made me dizzy but I couldn't think about myself. I needed to be super cool, feet on the ground. I'd never dealt with anything like this before.

'C'mon, Thomas, let's get you inside.'

When I helped him out of the car, he lent heavily. I had one arm around his waist as we climbed the stairs, and I held onto the rail with the other one to balance myself. He was bigger than me and his arm was like a lump of lead slung over my shoulder. He had a tendency to topple backwards with each step. I feared we'd fall, especially when we were climbing the thirteen backstairs. I struggled to tilt him forwards. I needed the help of angels and all the company of heaven.

Once inside the house, we headed towards the bedroom and he spread out on the bed.

I said, 'Would you like a cuppa?'

'Yes, sweetheart, thank you.'

I walked into the kitchen to boil the jug. What Thomas had done had been dangerous. What if it'd gone wrong?

I handed him his cup of tea. 'Here you are. You need to make an appointment with Dr F on Monday.'

'No. You can't tell anyone.'

'But you need help.'

'You have to promise you won't tell anyone. Anyway, it was your fault. You made me do it.'

"Me? What did I do?'

'You know.' He shrugged.

'I promise not to tell anyone as long as you promise you'll never try anything like that again.'

In bed, in the velvet quiet that night, I listened to Thomas breathe. It was three o'clock in the morning. Thomas's every breath seemed more important than his last. He could've gone too far. What if there'd been no breath when -? What if? I wept inwardly. How did I - how did we - get here?

The potential scenarios played over and over. I saw us falling backwards down the stairs with his heavy weight on top of mine. I pulled the blanket over my head and tried to unsee the day. I had to get a grip.

We still hadn't linked up with a church. Thomas had been unsettled without one. As a trained singer and keen chorister, Thomas was looking for a choir. Some of his rail modelling mates recommended different churches.

We started with the local Anglican. It was High Church, so different to Sydney's evangelical Low Church. We worshipped there a couple of times but the incense made me sneeze and gave me thumping headaches.

A few doors along from the Anglican church was the Uniting Church. It was a less imposing modern building set unassumingly into the side of a sloping suburban block. Inside the building was an empty honey coloured wooden cross hanging above the altar. The whole atmosphere was new territory for me but not so for Thomas, who'd been brought up Methodist. He'd been told that the church had a talented organist. She was a music teacher and her husband was the choirmaster. The choirmaster just happened to be a newly converted train enthusiast and he was about the same age as Thomas. So it was settled. We became regular communicants at a branch of the Uniting Church.

During one of our first visits, an elder came out to the front of the church and announced that while the minister was away, a locum would take the service.

A well-groomed middle-aged woman walked up and stood in front of the low, sleek, honey-toned altar. She smiled and said, 'Let us pray.'

I heard nothing of the prayer. I was too distracted. A woman? I glanced around at the congregation. No one seemed perturbed. A woman?

She was halfway through the sermon before I recognised my own prejudice. While on one hand I was happy to spout women's rights, yet here I was rejecting a pastor based on narrow beliefs and on teachings that women should be silent in church. Gender equality was not equating with my beliefs. Yet change was standing there in front of me in high heels, lipstick and a light blue slack suit.

How come she was allowed when St Paul wrote in the scriptures, 'They are not allowed to speak but must be in submission as the law says.'

Whose law?

Corinthians 1. St Paul 'I do not permit a woman to teach or to assume authority over a man; she must be quiet.'

If that was true, I shouldn't be listening to the preacher but I liked what I heard. I oscillated between scripture and query - why should women be quiet in the church and at home? I was ashamed of my misogynistic narrow response. An internal gate creaked open. This time it stayed open long enough for new thought to rush in.

And, now, decades later, many Christian brides are still being carried over fundamentalist/evangelical thresholds by grooms every bit as blinkered as I was. I, along with my evangelical friends, vowed to hand over our independence to the head of the house believing it to be a scriptural law of St Paul's; a supposed protectiveness to cushion the female fundamentalist - a vaccination against the equality of the sexes.

At the end of the service, I shook the locum's hand, thanked her and tried to take courage and inspiration from our handshake. As I walked out of church, there was an unexpected thrill then another. I felt lighter in step when we walked towards the car. So a woman could be a pastor.

For weeks afterwards, I waded through past beliefs. My inner self paced backwards and forewards. I was aware of moving away from institutionalised religion, which surprisingly brought me closer to the divine. My forthright godmother had said to a budding bishop, 'We're all on the same road, Love - it doesn't matter who you are or what you believe. We all belong.'

I'd shared it in my journal because what my godmother had said sounded fair and kind. The God, the Christ in my heart, the holiness, the He, the She, was love and kind.

Before I married, my quest for holiness had been strong. It wasn't dinner table talk but a solitary walk during the early morning or late night quiet times. I'd not heard about the life of the contemplative but that was where I was headed. I'd choose a particular fruit of the spirit and meditate on it. In Galatians 5: 22-23: the fruits of the spirit were '... love, joy, peace, forebearance, kindness, goodness, faithfulness, gentleness and self-control.'

I'd scribble thoughts into my journal. It never laughed at me. It revealed things I didn't know about myself. For example, I said one thing and did another. I needed to watch my actions to ensure they matched my words. I discovered personal agendas and how I needed to be honest about myself with myself. Fortunately, my journal had a keen sense of humour and listened to my waffling without judgement.

# The School Fete

It was one of those perfect end of September spring days for St Patrick's school fete. In spite of the fact that many children came from homes where there was little money, stalls overflowed with imagination and enthusiasm. The church's solid foundation had been built out of generations of struggling but generous hearts.

I arrived at the fete with Thomas around midday. Children ran up to say hello and showed trinkets they'd won at hoopla. There was a noticeable flurry at a tent nearby. The twelve by twelve tent was tucked into the side of the main building. Children waited in line, giggling and huddling, whispering to each other as if telling tales.

We walked over to the tent and peered in but there was nothing to see, just some plastic white cups laid out on a card table. Some children were holding the cups and stood talking in the closed front right-hand corner of the tent. I overheard Head Sister telling them to stay inside until they'd finished their drink.

Inside the tent there was an area curtained off and only the front section was visible. A few children lined up, waiting to go behind the curtain. Children jumped around in anticipation. I sensed Sister was blocking our entry or maybe I misread her security guard stance. We chatted a little until she indicated it was time for us to move on.

When Sister saw us, she smiled. She looked happier than I'd ever seen her. It hadn't taken long to realise I was teaching in a school under the authority of an out-of-control nun. I'd complained to Thomas about her antics and here I was introducing them to one another and she appeared to be a most amiable soul.

After buying a couple of hot dogs with tomato sauce and onions dripping down the sides, we sat on seats set up along a narrow strip of lawn, beside the rough suggestion of a driveway, beside the potted playground.

Billy, the young warrior, came over. We were best friends now, now that he had my measure and I had his. He seemed to stagger a little and slurred when he spoke. He mentioned how tired he was, a little unusual for the time of day and for a highly strung overactive child. He stretched himself out on the lawn and fell asleep at my feet.

'That's odd,' I said to Thomas, who was busy noting that the tent still seemed unusually popular.

'There's something going on up there,' he said and he wandered off while I sat listening to Billy's boy snoring, his innocent face turned towards the midday sun.

A group of Billy's disciples gathered at his feet and they too went to sleep.

I wandered up to the tent. Sister stood there blocking the entrance.

'Whatever's for sale, Sister, it seems to be popular.'

She laughed and stood full height like a sentry guard. I noticed a group of parents huddled inside the right-hand corner of the tent. They held plastic takeaway cups similar to the ones I'd seen the young boys holding earlier.

Was it a Catholic thing? A private mass, perhaps? I suppose with me not being a Catholic meant I couldn't go in. I headed back to the young class warrior who was by now sitting up. He and his cousins talked and laughed. They compared notes about how drunk they were.

Big Ears joined in. 'So,' I said, 'that's why you fell asleep, Billy. Goodness me.'

One little fellow asked the other, 'Did you win anything?'

In old men's voices, they chorussed, 'Nah, ya' never win - y'can't win.'

At the time, I didn't know they were talking about the poker machine in the tent hidden from view behind one of the curtains.

By now, more parents had arrived. Some headed for the tent while others showed no interest. Monseigneur was nowhere to be seen. Someone said he was interstate on a four day retreat. It was a case of while the cat's away.

At morning tea the following Monday, and while Sister was busy in the counting house counting out her money, I asked if anyone noticed that some children might've been sold alcohol at the fete – that some were drunk at my feet and I suspected they'd spent most of their money in the tent.

Someone changed the subject. When there was a break, I added that it wasn't right to serve alcohol to children. Silence. Change of subject.

At lunchtime, sister burst into our tiny staffroom. She waved a piece of paper high above her head. The tent had made more money than any other stall.

'Now, we'll say nothing to Father when he gets back. The counting's done and I'm on the way to the bank.'

I asked, 'Sister, were children sold alcohol at the fete?'

Sister's laugh was too high-pitched and her retort too quick to be convincing.' Of course not. Of course not.'

After the door closed, the staff advised me in whispers, 'Don't get involved.'

'But who's protecting the children and their families? They hardly have any money –'

'Leave it alone. Father can't find out.'

'If we don't make a stand, does that mean we condone it?'

I'd met many do-gooders doing no good. Did I sound like one? I suspected I did but there was the mantra, 'The standard we walk past is the standard we accept.' In this environment, the inebriated young ones had it right. 'Ya can't win.'

I wrote a letter to the director – the priest who'd directly employed me and I suggested that poker machines and alcohol either shouldn't be allowed at school fetes where young children could imbibe or there needed to be supervision. I was unaware that alcohol and poker machines, especially in the poorer areas, were an important fundraiser and part of the culture of some orders. My letter must've caused a chuckle or two in head office.

I'd been holding back tears since I'd witnessed the way the locals at St Pats were sucked dry. When pressed, some gave their last cent to the church, equal to the widow's mite.

A few weeks after the fete, I drove out of the school grounds and couldn't hold back the tears any more. Earlier in the day, I'd sighted the low results of the school assessments. The low benchmarks were an outcome of institutionalised and politicised disadvantage.

I was furious. I pulled over because I couldn't see from crying. As I sat in the privacy of my car, I cried and thought I'd never stop. Of course, it wasn't just about the betrayal of children and their trusting faithful families. I cried about the way I'd been discounted in my marriage as well; low benchmarks with the blessings of church and state. I was every bit as trapped in an insitutionalised politicised trap as these families were trapped in poverty of spirit and I was equally as discounted by the church.

I stopped crying by focussing on the students. I had to focus on them, not myself. I counselled myself – you're not a miracle worker, not a social worker.

Some of my teaching friends had taught in underprivileged schools and I'd hear their despair at the entrenched discrimination where lively, bright students could only achieve a fraction of their abilities. I'd always taught in privileged schools. Now, I understood some of my teaching friends' despair. I learnt first-hand that the state and church had created an underclass by limiting resources, endorsed lack of opportunities and permitted unacceptable low benchmarks. They were the ultimate adjudicators of these young children and their families.

These students needed to believe in themselves, needed to be empowered. It didn't help that the rot in this school came from the head.

My passion for education couldn't eradicate the wilful construction of neglect. The exploding of entrenched clan wars, witnessed every day in the playground, and now less often in the classroom, became easier to understand. Some of these students' yokes were too heavy. They bore burdens of hopelessness carried by past generations; passed onto their young shoulders born down by harsh beatings of poverty and deprivation of power.

The students and their struggling, faith-keeping parents deserved better. They deserved respect and needed support and opportunities. They wanted what was best for their children, every bit as much as any parent who paid thousands of dollars a year for their child to sit at a desk of entitlement and privilege. Their parents were probably every bit as ignorant about the underprivileged as I was before I'd been exposed to it.

Until this time, I'd lived exclusively on Sydney's protective north shore, except for a short time teaching privileged students in the beautiful Southern Highlands. Both were places where trusty Truman would've felt at home with his symbolic picket fence and manicured lawns.

I hardly knew how to handle my creeping shame of past and present privilege. I'd come from a comfortable working-class background, with middle class benefits, before we knew anything about the rise of the middle class. I'd been blissfully ignorant of the needs and disadvantages of the likes of my brothers and sisters at St Pats. My well-meaning boss in Sydney had warned me that the working class town I was going to would be a cultural desert.

But it wasn't. It was a microcosm of our nation, and for me, it was a refiner's fire and an unlikely mentor. This industrial landscape was where I gained an essential education in the melting pot of paradox where dark versus light and poverty versed privilege in a sweaty palm of place.

# A Real Treat

The asphalt playground flexed from the heat and split from fatigue and injustice. This was Sister's playground, too. I'd been warned plenty of times to keep a low profile around her. 'She's an erratic volcano.' It was an excellent description of a well-known bully, running rampant, stamping mercilessly on tender shoots.

I'd been teaching there for a few months when there was great excitement. Funding had been granted for swimming lessons at the local pool. It was a real treat but when the children stood in line at morning assembly, Sister took it upon herself to inspect the piggledy lines of little disciples.

"Get out. Stand here.'

A young boy from my class stood in front of Sister, head down.

'You're not going swimming. You're a naughty boy. You're not in uniform.'

He wasn't wearing regular sneaker type sports shoes. Instead, he wore plain black school shoes and he wasn't the only one.

'Excuse me, Sister, I have a note from P's mother asking if he could be excused for not wearing his sports shoes today.' I walked up to her and whispered, 'She said he's grown out of them and she'll buy him some new ones at the end of the week when she gets paid.'

'Hah!' Sister announced to all within hearing distance, 'You know she's a de facto. Five children - a de facto. Heaven knows who this one's father is.'

The child bowed his head. I hope he didn't understand her bias in the term de facto and I hoped he knew who his father was. I'd turned my back on the children, trying not to involve them.

'With respect, Sister, that's nothing to do with –'

'It's everything to do with –'

Sister was combative, with no regard for the children standing rigid nearby, heads bowed, trying to look invisible. They didn't want to be next. The young boy stood under the weight of shame over which he had no say. He was being held to account for his mother's marital status, a busy mother who'd been responsible enough to write a note and whose children were always clean and well mannered.

The class had been so excited about swimming. It was hard for them to stand still but with the thought of P not being allowed to go, their feet froze. Who'd be next? Meanwhile, they could hear other classes walking to the main gate because the buses had arrived.

'Sister,' I whispered, 'could I talk to you, please? Maybe in your office?'

She turned on her heels. 'Follow me.'

We walked into the excuse of an office, spartan and barely big enough to turn around. We didn't sit down. This wouldn't take long. It was a risk but it had to be said. If it wasn't now, when? Warning to shivering self – stick to the facts. Keep it simple. Plain English.

'Sister, Timothy also doesn't have the right shoes. His mother didn't write a note. It's unfair.'

Before I could finish, Sister slammed the office door so hard I was surprised that the glass panel in the top half of the door survived without so much as a hairline crack. We stood in a heat box with temperatures rising.

Sister said, 'Tim's father is the local bank manager – lovely family – comes from a good home.'

"Well, if P can't go swimming and you say T can, as far as I'm concerned no one in my class is going'

'How dare you speak to me like that.'

I'd had my share of responsibilities in the past. I couldn't stand by and let an innocent child be discriminated against in such a humiliating fashion. My knees wanted to buckle. "If P can't go and T can –'

Sister waved out-out. She hissed, 'They'll miss the bus if you keep standing there wasting my time.'

This school on the hill had been my first experience teaching in the Catholic system. I hadn't appreciated there were different Orders with different missions. This particular order was to serve and support the poor, especially women and children.

Sister M, the middle-aged deputy, with whom I'd made friends, was expecting a move at any time. She'd finished her degree and was unsure of her next placement. She'd requested to live in the community; no longer in a convent.

The end of the year was close. On the quiet, she explained to me how she was tied to her order and couldn't change but I could request a transfer to a school of another order. She suggested the Dominicans, known for their commitment to education and scholarship, and who acted out their faith through words and actions. She said I needn't go through Head Sister. She'd sign my request.

So the following year I transferred to a Dominican-run school led by an inspiring Head Sister D. The love and compassion in that school was palpable the minute I stepped through the front gate, into the staffroom, into the classroom.

The fourth grade students I taught had similar socio economic backgrounds to my previous students, but there was love and support from the very top. Getting to know these students and staff made me feel at home for the first time since my move.

Head Sister always started the day with a bright greeting. She was sunshine herself and lifted the teachers' spirits as well as the students. We stood in morning assembly lines in the large well shaded lunch shelter and Sister D would ask the children if anyone knew who needed our prayers. Some mornings, no prayers were needed. Other mornings, and eager hand would go up.

'Mummy's in hospital. She's getting a baby.'

'Poppy's really sick.'

So, we'd bow our heads and send love to Mummy and Poppy.

After announcements, Sister would turn to the students and tell them to go and have a great day. The students would walk, sometimes chat and skip to class in the knowledge they were much loved, safe and secure.

One lunch hour when I was on playground duty, one of my students came and sat beside me. He was well liked and usually sat with friends but today he sat next to me. I noticed he didn't have any lunch. He said he'd forgotten it, so I gave him some of mine. Next day, next lunch hour, the same.

He sat down with head held down. He spoke so low I could hardly hear him. He said, 'Mummy's sick and there's no food. Daddy's away.' J was big for his age and probably ate more than his share. He was one of five. He kept looking down to the playground for help.

My heart went out to him and we shared lunch again.

I'd never come across this situation before. What should I do? I knew his mother liked cooking so that afternoon I bought $30 worth of flour, butter, eggs, sugar, mixed fruit, fruit and some veg and a card with, 'Hope you feel better soon.' I knocked on the front door a couple of times but no one answered so I left the box on the doorstep.

Next morning, Sister D sent a message for me to see her in her office at the beginning of recess.

'I've just had a call from J's mother. She was in tears.'

"Is she okay? J said she's sick.'

'Anne, you meant well but before you do something like that in future, run it past me.' Sister was blushing. She looked every bit as uncomfortable as I was beginning to feel. 'People have their pride and Mrs S is a very proud Greek woman.'

'I'm not too sure I –'

'I assured her you meant well but – put it this way, if it was another person, she could've been insulted.'

I'd insulted her? Really? When I was growing up, we always shared and helped one another: eggs, veggies, second-hand clothing, maybe a chook or two.

'I'm sorry, Sister. I didn't mean to - should I go and apologise?'

'Let's say it was a generous gesture but inappropriate.'

'He was so hungry. What should I have-'

I hadn't thought to mention it to Head Sister. I thought I'd quietly drop off a few goods which might help. Of course, on reflection, I should've reported it. I wasn't a social worker. I had a lot to learn in this culture.

Head Sister said, 'If something like that happens again, and it will in an area like this, come and tell me and we'll do a home visit and take it from there. At least, now we know she's sick and her husband's away so we'll-'

'Sorry, Sister. I had no idea.'

The creep of embarrassment is as acute today as it was back then. I would learn, in time, of less patronising ways to help. I disliked being patronised and yet here I'd just upset a caring Greek mother.

About two weeks later, just as the lunch bell rang, J's mother appeared at the classroom door. She'd brought in a beautiful sponge cake for the class to share. It was my first opportunity to apologise. I attempted to. She reached out, touched my arm and thanked me, which made me feel worse.

At the end of the year, Johnny gave me a beautifully wrapped present. He asked me to open it in front of the class, something I usually avoided, but I sensed it was important to him and perhaps important to his mother.

I unwrapped the largish parcel to find a box containing a set of delicately embossed parfait glasses. There was a smaller box, too. It contained a set of sculptured long elegant parfait spoons, which I still use today. The card was filled with best wishes. This gift was worth far more than my earlier offering.

Eighteenth-century preacher John Wesley said, 'Do all the good that you can.' While I'd learnt to follow such a creed, I was now aware that it was possible to overstep the mark, to risk hubris; another fine line to be aware of along with the other subtleties of this culture.

The misunderstanding made me homesick for family and a familiar way of life where I understood the currency of manners. The more I stepped out of my comfort zone in this new town, the more I winced at my ignorant, seemingly arrogant self.

# Stirrups

It was lunchtime when I walked out of the staffroom. I'd booked in to have another fertility test and planned to leave school at lunchtime.

Head Sister D caught up with me, her head held down in her determined way. She stood by the front gate frowning. Her arms hugged herself. 'I don't like it. You should be going into hospital for this procedure. I don't like this at all.'

I was unaware at the time that my gyno was a well-known Catholic doctor and Head Sister was not impressed.

'You're not to come in tomorrow. I forbid it. I don't want to see you again until next week. Keep your feet up and rest. We'll be praying for you.'

The test had something to do with the lining of the womb. A neighbour said it sounded very much like a test she'd had but she'd stayed in hospital for a couple of days because there was risk of haemorrhage. She was the only woman I knew who undergone full-scale fertility tests.

The aftermath of each of my tests so far was blood, pain and no answers. Before the procedure, I was to take a tablet. It would've helped if Dr C had told me that the tablet would super-relax my muscles. I had a susceptibility to anything that caused drowsiness, which explained why I had trouble keeping my eyes open as I drove from school to the obstetrician's rooms up town.

I parked the car and struggled to climb out. I stumbled across the road to a row of terraces. Rang the bell. Stepped inside. Little said. On a bed. Injections. Chilly clink of instruments. Specialist gone.

The receptionist came in and linked arms with me and helped me sit up on the side of the bed. My whole body shook. She brought in a lovely cup of tea, which I tried to drink without spilling. I really needed to lie down and go to sleep.

After a while, the receptionist took me into the empty waiting room. She said, 'You'll need to sit here for about an hour. We don't want any complications, do we.'

I wished she'd left me lying on the bed for that hour. I sat on the cold chair and drifted in and out of oblivion.

Soon the receptionist packed up her desk, getting ready to go home. She said, 'Who's picking you up?'

'No one. I assumed I could drive.'

She shook her head as if she was annoyed with someone. I hoped it wasn't me.

'When you go home, if you have any problems, like excessive bleeding, go straight to hospital. You'd better sit here a bit longer. Would it be worth ringing your husband?'

"He's probably not in the office. His work's only five minutes away. I can go there. I'll be fine.'

The thing about this town, everything was only five minutes away so I drove, mustering all possible focus, to Thomas's work only a few kilometres away. I arrived at the office and parked under the faithful old shade tree. I wasn't thinking too clearly but knew I desperately needed my bed and I needed sleep. I'd intended to go into reception and ask for Thomas but I couldn't move. I was in a vice and a bloody mess. I looked around wondering if I could see anybody from the office who could go in and tell Thomas I was outside.

I couldn't believe it when I looked up and saw Thomas walking back from the depot to the main office. I waved and he came over looking puzzled.

"What's going on?'

I burst into tears. 'Can you drive me home, please?'

'Of course, sweetheart, of course.'

I reeled from the brutal rawness of the afternoon. Head Sister was right. This was a procedure that needed to have been done in hospital.

For the specialist, it was simply another day at the office, another fertility test; the results being of far more interest to him than my person.

In this industrial city, a sense of winter and the feeling of abandonment had seeped in and chilled my bones. These days, I wore extra layers of clothing because I'd lost so much weight and felt cold all the time. Usually, I loved winter, where I imagined I'd sit slipper-comfy by the fire. I pined for hand-in-hand soulmating.

As Thomas helped me up our back steps and after I curled up into the bed and rocked my pain to sleep, I mourned my apparent loss of self. There didn't seem to be much of me left.

At times like this, I'd prod Thomas. 'When can we go back? We've been here more than two years.'

'I don't know. It's not up to me.'

'But didn't you say we could go back after two years?'

'There's nothing available.'

'But if they said two years, shouldn't they keep to that?'

That was when Thomas would huff and puff, fold his arms and disappear into the recliner.

Since we'd moved north, I'd made good friends, loved my work and enjoyed the company of my colleagues and I'd started to paint again. I loved the garden and tried to maintain the gorgeous three-tiered colourful garden out the front. We had rich fellowship with our church friends and choir members. It wasn't like everything had fallen apart. I focussed on the things that worked and was thankful. Sometimes, that was hard work.

I used to sit out the back on our north-facing indoor/outdoor room and simply be. I'd take in the wide sweep of yard. I'd imagine our recently planted eucalypts as mature trees. Sometimes, Nanna sat there in spirit with me. In the silence, I could hear her say her favourite benediction: 'May the peace of God, which passes all understanding, keep your heart and mind in the knowledge and love of God.'

Nanna used to say that deep peace was possible regardless of what went on around you; be grateful and trust in the moment, but these days, it was almost too hard. This place had so many dimensions.

I looked out at the two huge weeping willows which wept into our backyard from a neighbour's yard. The willows provided much needed shade in summer. When the wind picked up their branches, the leaves cheered. Their cheering rose like the swell of a crowd.

When we sat watching TV one night, Thomas said he planned to go away for a weekend train trip, this time with a Sydney train friend. He said, 'I've organised for you to stay with Prue while Evan and I go on the trip. I'll get out of work early.'

'Do you mean this weekend?'

'Yes.'

'Like, tomorrow?'

'Yes.'

'I won't be able to. I'm having another test done after school. I have to take it easy when I get home.'

'But Pru's expecting you.'

'She'll understand.'

'You like Pru. You like going there.'

'I do but I'll need to keep my feet up.'

'Look, we can pack the car before we go to work. I'll meet you at the place. Where is it?'

'Uptown somewhere. I'm sure to run late, so don't worry. I'll be fine.'

Thomas insisted. Whenever Thomas insisted there was no way out, other than being caught in one of his rip tides, and that'd involve an element of risk.

As predicted, the specialist ran late, which meant I was late coming out. Thomas paced the near empty waiting room.

When I came out, he said in front of the receptionist, as if it was both our faults, 'You're late. We have to get a move on.'

I walked out of the surgery unsteady on my feet. I reached out to hold onto Thomas's arm. I couldn't walk fast. Thomas started to run between peak-hour traffic on the busy city road intent on beating the traffic lights.

I let go of his arm. 'I can't. You go.'

How could I explain to him what I'd been through? It was unimaginable. Legs up in stirrups. White-coated strangers, like miners with mining lamps, disappearing into the unknowable while nurses stood in silence beside me. Occasionally, they'd look at one another and then look down at me.

One whispered, 'Are you okay?'

'I'm alive.' I grimaced and we smiled.

We were all in this together. Only a woman would understand the indignity that accompanied this test.

The other nurse patted my hand and said, 'Nearly done... you're doing well.'

These fertility tests belong to an ancient world.

When Thomas reached the other side of the road, he turned and waved his hand for me to hurry. I shook my head. I stood in the middle of the busy road and waited for the lights to change.

I called out, 'Thomas, you go. I'm done.'

He waited for me to cross then we reached the car.

In the car, I said, 'Please drop me home. I need painkillers. I have to sleep.'

What I really needed was for my husband to take me inside, tuck me into bed, bring me some painkillers, some fresh pads, and make me a hot cup of tea. That was all I needed and then he could go away forever if he wanted.

He ignored my pleas and held the steering wheel knuckle-white tight and lead-footed down the highway weaving in and out of peak hour traffic. I shut my eyes as Thomas's fury overtook lines of weekend cars heading south on a late Friday afternoon. He ignored double yellow lines. He made it clear that I was the cause of the risks he had to take.

Every time I opened my eyes, I saw we were low-flying. I'd close them again and pray that the angels were with us. If there was to be an accident, I didn't want to see it. I sat beyond care, simply being and praying.

When we arrived at the railway station, Thomas pointed out that the train was already at the platform. 'Ready to depart. Gotta go.' He grabbed his bag and ran.

I moved guardedly across to the driver's seat. I looked for Thomas in the rear vision mirror and watched him craze his way through a crowded turnstile.

As soon as he was out of sight, I had the urge to put my foot on the accelerator and drive away, never to return, but reality controlled the steering wheel and led me to Pru's place. The angel took one look at me and put me to bed. She said it brought back memories for her, of the many times when her children were small when Evan went on train weekends. One time, she said, it was only hours after she'd arrived home from hospital, after having a hysterectomy.

Prue understood first-hand the heavyweight of abandonment. She spoiled me and pre-empted my every need. I slept, ate and we sat in the sun, talked then I went inside and slept some more.

When I next saw the obstetrician a few weeks later, he was keen to conduct further fertility tests. He said, 'My preference is that you have a curette every three months. It'll keep your womb in tip-top condition.'

I was tempted to say, 'I'm not an engine and I don't need a regular service,' but instead I said, 'I won't be doing any more tests, thank you.'

He was less than impressed. It seems unbelievable now that, at no point in those two years of invasive, expensive fertility tests was my husband's sperm tested. Didn't the specialist know it took two to tango? Male fertility tests were less invasive, less expensive, no blood shed, no pain, so why hadn't Thomas's sperm been tested first?

My GP had referred me to him. He said he was the leading fertility specialist in the area. In retrospect, his opinion could've been a little biased coming out of the mouth of another small, compact, middle-aged Scot; the difference between them being that my doctor was a gentleman and cared.

He was surprised when I refused to go back and see 'that callous man' and referred me to a younger obstetrician. No procedures this time; only investigations. I was put on hormone treatment for twelve months. The tiny pill stabilised me – brought back my weight and hormone stability. I felt so good.

During those years of tests, I was unaware that my mother-in-law had mentioned to my mother, but not to me, that Thomas had had a severe case of mumps in the testes when he was fourteen, which could possibly cause damage or low sperm count.

My mother-in-law said, 'I told your mother about it. I was worried. I knew you wanted to have children.'

'Why didn't you tell me?'

'Because I thought it was more a mother-daughter thing. Can you imagine if you'd called off the engagement and Thomas found out that I'd spoken to you? I would've been blamed – you know what that would've been like.'

'I do.'

One day I said to Thomas, 'Did you know that when you had mumps it could've affected your fertility?'

'No.'

'I didn't know either.'

When I asked Mum why she hadn't told me what June had said, she said, 'It shouldn't make any difference. You either love them or you don't.'

# The Right Order

The extra vitamin E tablets Thomas had taken, the baggy cotton underpants he'd been advised to wear and our strict adherence to the daily temperature chart, made no difference to my fertility stakes. The fact that nothing happened carried with it a heavy yoke which couldn't be ignored, so I suggested we enquire about adoption.

Thomas said, 'I don't mind either way. I'm happy with just the two of us, but if you want to, go ahead.'

The adoption process proved to be like conception in the public domain; almost as shameful as copulating in public. It fuelled nervous energy.

Thomas worried whether we had intercourse often enough. 'Do you know?'

I doubted it. I said we were probably average but in reality I often wondered what on earth I'd 'saved' myself for.

I was worried more about if I/we'd be good enough. Would there be a match? And what about the 'biological mother,' as we were taught to call her. My hair stood on end when I first heard that label; so cold, so impersonal. How could I possibly take her place – her heartbeat, her quickening pulse, the sounds and smell of her body? How was it possible to celebrate the birth of a new soul while the young mother had to bear such loss and walk away with empty arms? The ache of empty arms after each of my miscarriages gnawed at my soul. How would the mother cope with the pain of weeping full breasts when her milk came in?

We'd been warned that the adoption process was a long emotional labour. That was an understatement starting with a mind-boggling-baby-might-come-maybe-next-month-maybe-next-year.

A meeting was held at a hospital where adoptee parents met in a small waiting room. It was hard to know where to look. Embarrassment and disappointment drowned every conversation. People apologised for being there as if they'd done something wrong. There were subtle ripples of sympathetic folding and unfolding of arms and legs. Half-smiles were passed around, aimed more at the room than any particular person. Eyes revealed the pain of years of disappointments, barren monthly cycles, unwanted bleeds.

The social worker appeared in the doorway and ushered us into an even more dingy room which looked and felt sad, or was that my imagination?

She listed requirements. '...and you'll need character references from a minister of religion and another one from a respected citizen.'

While none of us were ministers of religion, I assumed we were all respected citizens. I was tempted to be flippant about it to ease the tension in the room but feared the social worker might put a black mark against my name or put us at the end of the queue or, worse still, drop us off the queue altogether for being less than perfect.

'And you'll have to make a substantial financial contribution.'

The interview stripped us naked well before the home visit. Some couples dropped out. After our adoption application was approved, we waited. I wondered how the average respected citizen would feel if each time, before giving birth, they had to follow a similar regime; provide character references and undergo an inspection by authorities to check on the child's environment. Nerve-wracking as it was, it made perfect sense. These were precious souls coming into the world and they deserved the best.

A few months after the first appointment with the adoption agency, I was elated when I fell pregnant. I rang the social worker immediately and told her. She suggested we leave our names on the list for now. I didn't like the sound of that. It suggested she expected something untoward would happen. I found it hard to believe God would allow that.

At the time, a pumpkin vine grew in our backyard and I'd become quite attached to it. I hadn't realised they were so beautiful. I remember sitting down beside the vine early one morning, when the leaves were still dove-grey in the soft light, and it shone like velvet with dewdrops. Its voluptuous leaves and glorious golden flowers faced the sun sending out a clear clarion call to Mother Nature.

When I was young, pumpkin vines sometimes grew in our backyard but I'd never noticed their beauty. To brush up against their leaves when playing, tiny spikes stung and itched the skin, so I'd learnt to keep away from them, until now.

I'd been unsettled about this pregnancy, although preparation for the baby's nursery continued. I knitted mostly white and lemon baby's clothes. I'd embroidered some of them with lemon and white tiny rabbits and mice. They looked like Beatrix Potter's Peter Rabbit and Hunka Munka. Morning sickness kept every stitch company.

It was the eleventh week when I started to spot. By week fourteen, the spotting increased, so the gynaecologist sent samples away for tests. He assured me spotting was nothing to worry about. I believed him - that is, until I had a vivid dream.

*A pumpin vine grows in our backyard. It's thick, lush, dew-dropped. Leaves sway in the breeze. Golden flowers gleam. Leaves circle. The circle tightens. Too tight. Everything speeds, spins. The circle shrinks. Golden trumpets and voluminous leaves shrivel and drop. Instead of a flourishing vine I see a ring of stinking mush. A dark stain on the grass. I wake, knowing.*

It was the sixteenth week and I was to sing a small solo with the choir at the Sunday morning service. As I turned to walk out of the bedroom, I felt a sudden rip. I crouched over hoping to ease the pain and said to Thomas, 'I don't think I can go - the pain.'

'You have to.'

'I know but I can hardly stand.'

'It'll wear off.'

'I hope so. I don't like it.'

After taking a mild painkiller, we arrived at church.

An older member of the choir saw me coming awkwardly down the front steps, nursing my anxiety. She hurried over and put her arm through mine. 'By the looks of you, you should be in bed,' and she directed me towards one of the back pews. She whispered, 'I don't care what he says, you stay here.'

Excused from choir, I sat with the congregation while Thomas sent me looks of disapproval when another soprano sang my small solo. The look said, you've let me down - again. By the time we got home, there was wet pain and I shivered.

I rang Mum.

She said, 'I don't know what to say. I never had any trouble... keep your feet up.'

'I have an appointment with the specialist tomorrow. I hope he can tell me what's going on.'

'... make sure you keep your feet up.'

I went to bed and propped up my feet.

Next morning, the pain was stronger and there was more determined spotting caused by a tug-o'-war between Mother Nature and me. When I drove Thomas to the bus stop, I tried to tell him about my fear of losing our baby but there was no time. The bus was there, waiting.

He kissed me and said, 'I'll ring you later - see how you got on. You'll be fine.'

Nothing, absolutely nothing, was fine. My pain level changed instantly. I couldn't update Thomas on the loss of blood because we couldn't talk about blood, not since he nearly fainted during a shoot-out in *Bonnie and Clyde,* one of the films he came to see with me when I studied film.

I needed a big strong comforting life-giving hug. Instead, I listened to the bus tsss as it pulled away. My energy drained. I turned the car around and drove to our local GP. I walked in slowly so as to keep movements to a minimum. Dr F rang the obstetrician, who said for me to go to hospital straight away. They'd be expecting me.

The GP offered to ring an ambulance.

'Thank you but I came in the car. I'll ring Thomas when I get home.'

'Promise me you'll go straight home, ring your husband and get to hospital as soon as you can.'

'Yes.'

My intention was to do just that. I climbed into the car and felt the whole world collapse in my lap; into the lap of an utter failure. Fear and grief didn't hide anything from me. They raged; frenetic palpitations drummed all the way home.

Inside the house, I stood in the corridor of irrational thinking, incapable of logic. I clung to hope because sometimes in the past impossibility thinking had worked. My instructions to self were simple - do everything in the right order.

I rang Thomas's work.

Someone said, 'Sorry, love. He's out of the office. He should be back any minute. I'll tell him you rang.'

'Can you tell him it's urgent, please.'

I fed the dog and cat, packed a small bag and hoped Thomas would ring, but, no, so I rang my neighbour, a good friend, and explained the urgency.

'Of course, of course, I'll take you.'

'Thank you. I'll wait up by the letter box.'

'No, pop down. I have to get ready.'

In my world, responding to an emergency was to pop on shoes, grab keys and purse and be there within minutes.

I assumed that Jill, being a woman with four children, would grasp the urgency by its tail and swing into action. But, as she'd never miscarried she seemed unaware that my problems were bad news at sixteen weeks.

As I headed out of the house, I spoke to my unborn child. 'I'm sorry. This is not okay but I'll look after you, don't worry. Don't worry.' This was definitely not okay. I walked down the front steps, saying, 'I'm sorry, I'm sorry.' I felt sorry for even being alive.

I took extra small steps as I made my way up our steep drive. Jill only lived two doors down but today her place seemed miles away.

When I reached the front door, it was open and she called out, 'Come in, come in. I'm having a quick shower. Won't be long.'

A shower? Was she kidding?

I walked through the house and sat on a tall stool in the kitchen. I chose the stool closest to the back door so I could look out and distract myself. My self talk wasn't great - silly silly girl - why didn't you let the doctor ring for an ambulance? - silly girl. Thomas could've picked up the car later - you've brought this on yourself - silly silly girl. And, what would Dr F think if he saw you - silly girl - sitting here in your friend's kitchen as if you don't have a worry in the world?'

But if I rang for an ambulance now, Jill might be offended. Her persona was that of Earth Mother of four and Earth Mother had declared she needed a shower. Who was I to say no, you can't do that, but I needed to go now.

I tried to distract myself with the cats. I could see they'd spilt some of their wet food onto the newspaper which was spread out under their feeding bowls near the stove. I imagined the smell of cat food under fingernails and felt sick. I glanced towards the kitchen window for help. All I could see was next door's brick wall.

Jill? Where was Jill? Didn't she know there was a formidable force out of control in her kitchen?

I walked into the hallway and called out, 'Jill, I'll ring an ambulance. It'll be easier.'

She popped her head out of the bathroom. She was dressed and towelling her hair. 'Hang on. Would you like a cuppa? I need one.'

'No, thanks. I have to get to hospital. They're expecting me. I'll ring an ambulance. That'll save-'

'No, no, no. Look, I'm almost ready.' She made a cuppa and sat on a stool opposite me and waved towards the piles of washing. 'I need to separate the coloureds from the whites. It won't take a minute. I can put on a load of whites.'

My friend's sense of urgency was maddening. Every second was too long. I teared up.

She stood up and said, 'C'mon, you'll be right. It won't take long, honest.'

I'd forgotten it was Monday, Jill's washing day; the whirlpool of her week. Piles of clothes waited to be sorted into piles outside the laundry. As my friend separated the coloureds from the whites, I noticed she moved with more deliberation than usual. I feared this emergency had disoriented her. Maybe she struggled to keep her world on its axis. Did she think that if she did everything in the right order, she could stop something bad from happening?

I projected, of course. That was me. I did things like that all the time. Frustrated as I was with Jill, I understood. Whenever I needed to ground myself, I'd focus on order. I watched my friend order her world into coloureds and whites while I attempted to keep Mother Earth, the Solar System and the Universe on track.

# Life and Death

Jill and I arrived at Emergency.

Someone from the hospital hurried over to the car and said, 'You can't park here.'

Jill explained my position, so they called for an orderly to bring a wheelchair. I was wheeled into the reception area.

The receptionist peered over. 'We were expecting you ages ago.'

'I'm sorry.'

'There's a room,' and she gave directions to the orderly and a nurse accompanied us to a small dark room and I climbed up onto a firm cold bed.

A little while later, the nurse walked in and took my vitals. No eye contact, no greeting. As she left the room she called back, 'Doctor's in surgery. Meantime, rest up.'

Sister appeared some time later with the specialist. The looks she shared with the doctor, when he patted my blanketed knee, made me suspect she knew more than I did. I'd been told nothing but deep down my gut knew everything.

The obstetrician said, 'I'm going to admit you to keep the neighbours happy. They can't say we're not looking after you.'

He and Sister shared knowing looks.

I said, 'I was meant to see you today to get my test results. Did they show anything?'

He tapped my knee again. 'You're in good hands. Let's just wait and see.'

They left the room in whispers. What he wasn't telling me, an what he could've, and should've, told me was that the results showed the foetus wasn't developing normally. Unbeknowns to me, he'd already written 'inevitable abortion' on my chart. I would read that later, after the fact.

The good Catholic doctor made the decision to hand me over to Mother Nature. She worked hard for two days. On the third day, the situation deteriorated quickly to the extent I haemorrhaged and went into shock. I shivered and heard someone screaming. I knew exactly how she felt. I sent her one of my incomprehensible prayers. I turned and asked Sister what was wrong with her.

She patted my hand. 'There's no one, dear.'

I felt a strong presence to my right. It appeared as a gentle misty form of light. Pure essence. My first thought was Jesus. I felt that if I reached out, I'd be able to touch Him.

The nuns and I'd been praying our own silent prayers. I knew first-hand its power. And here was Love answering prayers in amongst this bloody mess.

Curtains were drawn. Additional sheets arrived.

Sister looked visibly upset and started to pat my hand faster and faster. 'Doctor's on his way. He's been difficult to get hold of.'

Thomas had been difficult to get hold of, too. He came to see me during his lunch break.

That's when I overheard the lady in the bed next to me whisper loudly to him, 'I'm sorry to hear she's losing the baby.' She told each of her visitors the same.

In the late afternoon, Dr C finally arrived. He saw the mess and winced. He apologised. In a matter of minutes, there was a needle and instant relief. The other woman, the one I heard, stopped crying too.

Sisters wrapped me in extra warm blankets. Their kindness and love was overwhelming.

By the time the middle-aged, balding porter arrived, I was subdued, super-thankful for pain relief.

He tried to cheer me up as he wheeled me to the lift. Once inside, he said, 'And what are you up to tonight, love?'

'I'm losing my baby.'

'Oh, I'm sorry. I shouldn't have-'

'You weren't to know.'

The mother-to-be in me had to face the reality and it took the porter to help me say it.

As we ascended to a higher floor, I knew I was leaving behind dreams and hopes. I stared at the layers of white thermal blankets that covered me. So Life and Death were warm and white.

When I was wheeled into the theatre, Dr C and his team gathered around. They'd been called together urgently and they chatted, obviously pleased to see one another. They lifted me across and placed me carefully onto the chilly, narrow bed. I tried to mirror their smiles but life was too raw. It was attempting to rip bloody clots out of me but I had nothing more to give.

The specialist led the camaraderie. I'd hoped there'd soon be quiet and a sense of reverence for the loss of my once promising bud. I needed the doctor to refrain from boasting about his golf scores before I went under. The last thing I saw was his full round face leaning over me telling me how much he looked forward to dinner. 'We're having curried sausages tonight.' Then I was gone.

When I woke in Recovery the aroma of his curried disrespect was still there. My bud and I deserved better.

The next day when I packed to go home, a doctor told me in a soft reassuring voice, 'You're one of the lucky ones.'

So, in the midst of a brand new day, I gave thanks for being born at a time and place with access to life-saving medical intervention.

Thomas arrived to take me home.

Sister wheeled me out to the car and chatted to both of us and said, 'How good it is to see the sun.'

As Thomas and I drove away, he said, 'I have to get back to work. We're in the middle of a major roster.'

I didn't care about rosters or what the rest of the world was doing. All I wanted to do was to crawl into my own bed and somehow come to terms with the enormity of what had just happened.

Six weeks later at my follow-up consultation with Dr C, I sat opposite the one whom, I realised, I no longer respected. He hardly acknowledged me when I walked in. He busied himself cutting and pasting notes into a manilla folder; pre-computer days.

'There's one good thing that's come out of this,' he said. 'We know now that you'll never have trouble carrying it full term.'

I wished he would stop calling my baby 'it.' But, of course, he referred to a less than perfect foetus. I knew that biologically it was a foetus but, emotionally and psychologically, I carried a living breathing perfectly formed pink chubby-faced bundle of joy.

'Did I have a boy or a girl?'

'A boy.'

'What went wrong?'

'The foetus didn't develop properly. Quite common.'

Still no eye contact, no commiserations. He looked at my notes and wrote some more.

I asked him, because I already knew the answer, 'Did you know that would happen when I first went into hospital?'

The pen faulted.

'I mean, did you know I was going to miscarry?'

'Abort? Yes.'

The unseen lioness in me prowled around his desk, looking for blood and a lost soul. 'So why, then, was I allowed to go through everything to the point of haemorrhage?'

No reply.

'I mean, I ended up- '

'Yes. It was a mass. A lump of flesh. It was never going to-'

Still no eye contact. He prepared to stand up by swivelling his chair, indicating to me that the consultation was over.

I stayed seated. Indignation and determination anchored me. I wasn't going anywhere until I had my say. 'As you know,' I said stunned at the strength of my growl, 'I had unbelievable pain and went into shock. I'd never want that to happen to anyone. If my results were what they were, then why wasn't I given a curette immediately?'

The specialist stood up and stepped back as if my claws had drawn blood.

I pressed. 'I'd like to know why.'

He moved around his desk and headed towards the door. 'It's too complicated to explain. I'd like to see you in three months, so make an appointment on your way out.' He opened the door.

I rose and, in an instant, he was no longer prey. I never wanted to see this insensitive man ever again. In essence, he curried favour with his own religious dogma at the expense of compassion and risking a mother's life.

After church the following Sunday, I didn't feel like talking to anyone. I didn't want sympathy from the few who knew so I hurried to the car.

As I climbed the steps, I heard urgent shouting. 'Anne, Anne, wait, wait.'

It was the woman who helped me lead Girls' Group. She belonged to a new Pentecostal subgroup in the church who believed that the rest of us were 'unsaved' because we didn't speak in tongues and didn't have the gift of prophecy, which they believed they had.

P ran up the last step of the steep path and stood there puffed. She grabbed both my hands and kissed me on each cheek. 'Terrible, terrible news but I want to share with you something that God has laid heavy on my heart. I know why you lost your baby. I feel led to tell you. You lost it because you're not right with the Lord.'

'Oh, really?' I spoke from a subterranean level of disbelief at her insensitivity. I sent back to her, 'So, I suppose all those billions of unbelievers who breed like rabbits are right with the Lord?'

'Oh, they don't count.'

I took my hands back, shook my head and climbed into the car. I started to count aloud one, two, three, four. I said to Thomas, who'd been standing waiting at the driver's door keen to go, 'Get me out of here before I explode.'

Here was another one currying favour with fundamentalist dogma at the expense of fundamental compassion.

I'd felt the presence of the Lord, of a higher power of Love, when I was in hospital. I was still warm from that holy hug and from being held in strong arms of prayer. The overwhelming warmth of spirit had been as strong and as real as the kind sisters who'd sat beside me.

Sometimes at the end of day, it was harder to carry the loss. It seemed so much heavier.

If I mentioned it to Thomas, he'd say, 'Sweetheart, put it out of your mind. It's not going to help if you keep thinking about it.'

But every cell in my body grieved. There was no hormonal grief button to turn on or off.

One night as we sat up in bed I asked Thomas, 'What if we referred to him as John? It's your middle name and your father's.'

Thomas put down his magazine and smiled. 'That's lovely. Okay.'

And that was the extent of our shared grieving.

I snuggled up to him while he read. I needed to keep warm. These days, I was always cold. Summer cotton sheets chilled my bones. I needed a winter blanket. I turned on the electric blanket to three and turned it off once I began to roast and soon fell asleep.

When I tried to talk to Mum about it on the phone, she'd stop me and say, in the kindest way, 'Look, let it go. There's nothing you can do. It won't do you any good thinking about it. I don't understand. I never had an ounce of trouble. Try to think about something else.'

I tried and one morning as I hung out the washing, my neighbour, who'd had a miscarriage earlier in the year, called out, 'How are you going? I was a mess when it happened. I cried for days... had to go to Mum's.'

So she'd cried too. Someone understood. I'd felt ashamed of crying all the time. I could've filled an ocean. I cried when I was alone making the bed, when I washed up, drove the car. I was so grateful to my neighbour for sharing, for helping me feel what I needed to feel.

As the hormones settled, I learnt to live with and around the grief. I found myself thinking more about the future. The way out of grief was to focus on the adoption. I rang the adoption agency and told the social worker what had happened.

Adoption was a difficult topic to bring into any conversation. It proved to be a highly emotive word spoken in hushed tones. Meanwhile, I kept busy as I rode the emotional and hormonal big dipper with the hope that one day, any day, maybe next month or next year, I'd become someone's mum.

# The Arrival

The day I received the phone call saying that our baby son had arrived turned an ordinary day into an extraordinary one. The day had been very ordinary. I'd just arrived home from school, had kicked off my shoes and put on the kettle. That's when the phone rang. At that time of day, I expected it to be either Mum or Thomas ringing me to say hello, during their afternoon tea break.

It was the social worker from the adoption agency. She said something like, 'Your baby boy has arrived,' or did she say, 'your baby son?'

He'd arrived. Our baby son had arrived. My baby hormones went wild. They were ready. Breasts throbbed from a recent biological memory. Our adopted son had arrived in the same week our biological son would've been due, around 1 November.

I rang Thomas. Rang Mum.

Rang the principal. 'Sorry, I can't come in tomorrow.'

I shook with fear, joy, anticipation. I called out to Jill from the back patio when I saw her bringing in the washing. 'He's arrived.'

Congratulations spread from back veranda to back veranda, across back fences. Due to our position in the crescent, we had seven neighbours backing onto our long large backyard.

Next thing, young mothers were out on their back verandas offering, 'Do you have bottles? Nappies?'

'Um.'

'I've got nappies,' someone called.

'She'll want to get her own.'

'What size is he?'

'I don't know.'

'What bottles do you need? I've got some in good condition.'
'I, um, ah-'
'What size teat? I have some unopened if you'd like them.'
'Um-'

Suggestions about teat sizes, bottles sizes, nappies, flew enthusiastically from back porch to back porch. I was overwhelmed to the point of tears. We laughed as the soft glow of the sinking afternoon sun shone on my back decking where I stood in the limelight and trembled.

I busied myself buying bottles and teats in the local chemist shop, the core of our small community. As customers heard the news, they came over and hugged me, congratulated me, gave me advice, wanted to know how, why, when and where.

Next morning, unbelievably, we stood on a train platform. I say unbelievably because I still can't believe it happened. Thomas, the new father, insisted we bring our baby son home by train. Of course, I expected we'd go by car. I'd packed the baby bag and the car basket and was ready to go when I got caught up in a boys' own adventure.

I felt helpless when I stood on the rail platform. Thomas had performed when I said I didn't want to go by train. If I'd continued to go against his will, the trip to Sydney would've been fearful. I'd experienced a few of those trips. It wasn't something I could cope with right now. I was shaking with anticipation and excitement.

While we waited for the train to arrive on the platform, Thomas sat the baby's car basket by his feet, close to the edge of the platform, close enough to invite concerned stares from waiting passengers.

Once in the train, Thomas reached up and put the baby basket into the luggage rack and sat down. He chuckled. 'You should see the expression on their faces.'

I wanted to stand up and reassure the passengers that there was no baby in the basket. I wanted to tell them I'd never do that. I wanted to say how sorry I was that they felt so anxious. There was nothing, nothing wonderful about sitting in a railway carriage trying to normalise a ridiculous situation.

When Thomas first mooted the train travel idea we were about to leave the house. I said, 'We can't do that. It's impractical.'

'I want to tell my son when he's older about his first train ride.'

'He's five weeks old. He'll never remember. It's impractical, too hard.'

My main concern was that our baby might fret for his foster mother or his biological mother so it might be hard to settle him. How could I warm up a bottle and change his nappy in a noisy crowded train? I couldn't think. Thomas had caught me off guard again.

I said, 'And, we'll have to catch a cab to Mum and Dad's. This is so impractical. Honestly, Thomas, this is - it's -'

Thomas laughed. 'Charlie's picking us up after.'

'Is he?'

Duped again. Arrangements had already been made.

Our son's biological mother had been reluctant to sign the adoption papers. She'd waited until the last day, the thirtieth day, to sign them. Since that time, we've learnt more about the distress and coercion young mothers faced. They were traumatised and forced to leave with empty arms. As adoptive parents, we knew nothing back then about these practices.

We climbed the stairs of an old two story building, an old rabbit warren. Our son had been in his foster-mother's care when we walked into the office the social worker introduced us. High and emotional. Everything and everyone dissolved into the background when the foster-mother smiled and handed him over to me. Frightening bliss.

As I held our beautiful baby son, my heart went out to him and his biological mother. I imagined him in her womb and her giving birth. She was one of our family, too, even though we'd never meet. Her son, our son, one of the many sons down the ages who are only ever here on loan to us, was five weeks old and alert. I wished she could see how intently he followed our voices, already trying to work things out.

I was relieved to learn that our son had been with a foster family for the past four weeks, in their family home in Willoughby, around the corner from where I grew up. Thankfully, he'd not been left in a busy hospital nursery. I assumed it was better for a baby's well-being, which it was, but I was saddened to learn years later that it was also a strategy to prevent conflict between the newborn's families should one of them arrive at the hospital with the intention of preventing an adoption and raising the child; a distressing scenario.

I changed the little darling's nappy before we left. I'd changed dozens of nappies before, having had a lot to do with nieces and nephews and I'd been a babysitter since I was fourteen. Even so, the emotion of the moment overwhelmed me and I thought I might faint.

Meanwhile, everyone chatted. My son looked up and listened as I spoke to him. We met in our own small universe, eye to quizzical eye. Thomas stood close by and smiled. He'd not had much to do with babies. When I put our son into his arms, he looked concerned.

'It's okay. You'll get used to it.'

The experienced foster-mother said in a practised quiet voice, 'He doesn't like noise. I have four noisy boys and he startles easily... a slow eater... mostly feeds at night - sorry, I haven't been able to change that... hasn't put on much weight... hasn't unclenched his hands... hasn't smiled.'

Immediate challenges. Thomas handed him back to me.

'Look,' the foster-mother said, 'he can't take his eyes off you. He's forgotten me already. What are you going to call him?'

'Paul.'

When she heard that, she beamed. 'I shouldn't have crossed his name out on his baby's card. That's what we called him.'

She handed me his clinic card. He'd been attending the same baby clinic I went to as a baby. Immediately, I had images of the inside of the clinic and how I used to sit beside my mother in the waiting room when my little sister went there. Yes, I could see already we had a connection, and in the interim, he'd had good care.

We said our goodbyes and left with our bundle of joy, no more a thought, a wish, a dream but now an amazing seven pound four reality. Oh, boy. Oh, boy. This was it.

When we stepped outside into the bright sunlight, Charlie stood there with a Cheshire grin. He was the other excited one in this boys' own adventure. He was the father of two children and knew all the baby talk. He took photos for our family album.

Soon we crossed the Harbour Bridge. I sat in the back with our son in his car basket beside me. He was unbelievably cute. His eyes were wide. I held his tiny silken hand and talked softly. I sang 'Twinkle twinkle.' His eyes never left mine. What was he thinking? Was he listening for a familiar voice, the one he'd heard in the womb? Did I sound similar? I wanted him to feel at home, to feel love, to one day connect with the divine in us all.

When we reached 39, there was a marvellous welcoming committee, with more to come after work. There was so much love in the room. I held Paul as he drank his bottle of baby's milk. A room full of his new family watched his every move. After he finished the bottle, I held him up and stroked his back and he burped on cue. Everyone cheered.

My brother and sister-in-law called in after work to pick up their children and to see their new nephew. When they heard we'd come down by train, my brother said, "We're driving you home.'

He insisted. To say I was relieved would be an understatement. Thomas's objections were outnumbered and the trip home became a happy family affair; a bonus – something that wouldn't have happened if we'd gone down by car.

It was at times like this I missed my family. I wanted our little one to know his grandparents' and extended family's love. I wanted him to become one in their ways.

When I held him, his intense gaze took me somewhere in the depths of the universe. While there, I promised him I'd be as committed to him and love him as I would've loved our natural born son had he gone full term. I hugged this precious soul who was meant to be here at this time, at this place.

I sent his birth-mother a spirit message. 'Have no fear. I'll love and care for this little darling to the best of my ability.'

Finally, it was my turn to become a full-time mum.

# Happy Nappy Valley

There were those in our crescent who excelled in bleaching nappies, whiter than white. Husbands were definitely not part of the scene. At first, I was oblivious to it but, as a new mother, I was soon alerted to the competition one day after I'd hung out my nappies quite late.

Jill called out one morning over the fences. 'Oh, goody, you get your nappies out even later than me. Do you soak them in bleach?'

Did she have to mention nappies? Three buckets, daily, full of nappies in varying degrees of stinky poo and soggy muck holding court in my laundry, before being promoted to the next most appropriate bucket in a line of buckets, my least favourite start to the day but, as my mother said with tongue in cheek, 'That's one of the joys of motherhood.'

I was too deep in creamy mustard-looking baby poo to agree.

'Mum, motherhood's not all joyful. It's agony and ecstasy.' I broke the golden rule by mentioning the existence of a messy poo-ridden stink in the sacred world of motherhood.

'How can you say such a thing?'

'Because my fingers stink.'

I was busy sterilising bottles, making up formula and, and, and –

Jill said, 'I put them out late. All part of the game.'

'What game?'

'As to who gets their nappies out first and whose are the whitest. I bags first prize for the latest and I don't care about the whitest. Some of my nappies are ancient.'

From then on, I couldn't help but watch neighbours' clotheslines. At one stage, I worked out that in our crescent we had seventy-six children under the age of sixteen. This world of domesticity was so new, so physically draining and so emotionally exhausting, I'd turn green with envy whenever I heard the neighbours' parents visiting, helping, washing, vacuuming, talking, laughing. I'd love to have had such easy access to, and support from, my parents.

I'd always found the look of washing on the line very appealing. It was the beautiful simplicity; a sacred cleansing for the family, but it was at those times, as a young mother at home hanging out the washing, hours away from family and with no daycare in town, that I longed to be closer.

Some months after our young son arrived, a couple of schools in which I'd taught rang and offered me work. It was tempting and Thomas approved. With the arrival of a young son, there were extra expenses. It would help meet some of the costs.

But babysitting was a problem. Head sister offered to help organise it. And so it was that, when our son was six months old, I headed off to school with bottles of milk and nappies and a stroller and toys, toys, toys. The sisters cooed and cared for him, taking him for walks, and often I had no idea where he was, which was incredibly unsettling.

"Oh, don't worry,' said one of the sisters at recess one day, 'a couple of sixth graders are walking him around the playground.'

What? Sixth graders out there in that jungle with my precious bundle? I raced out. He was safely strapped in his stroller and there was a small following of carers escorting him around the playground. But a lot can happen on a playground in a second or two.

The principal suggested, 'You can keep him in class with you if you like – we've talked about it and we have no objection.'

So I tried. For two weeks. The children loved it. My young son liked all the attention but I didn't like it. Instead, I pictured us at home sitting on a rug underneath the Japanese willow in the filtered morning sun. I could tell him all about the curling, swirling autumn leaves which fell onto the rug. We could watch the moving clouds paint pictures in the sky or watch an ant carry his groceries home. We could lie on our backs and look up and up and pretend to be a bird.

That week would be my last teaching post for the next year. I simply couldn't keep tearing myself apart.

When I did go back to part-time work, I bartered babysitting hours with a neighbour. One neighbour had a son a few months older than mine. She was a local with oodles of family support but was delighted to barter a few more hours of child-free time.

She prided herself on being a modern mum. I was to find out just how modern after the first day. She'd handed out cups of milky, generously sugared coffee to our highly stimulated two-year-olds.

When I said I preferred Paul to drink milk, that he was easily hyped, she laughed. 'That's sooo boring.'

Even so, I continued to provide boring supplies of milk and juice for drinkies, in vain. Coffee remained the modern mum's preference. By the time I arrived there to pick up an over-excited, over-tired toddler of an afternoon, I was usually functioning below ground level, and my son by that time was several feet above. I'd still be coaxing him to come down from the coffee chandelier at ten o'clock at night. Futile attempts.

At the end of a long exhausting day, with another and another coming up, I'd be coaxing my lively son to slumber with an extra long bath, wiping his face, eyelids, nose, mouth then after a slow relaxing wipe down there'd be more hot milk then a long, long desperation-made-up story about a little boy who was so, so tired but, no. Caffeine was both deaf and recalcitrant.

Part-time teaching didn't work. I needed to be there to fill my son's cup with full cream milk. There was no day care, only a local preschool for four-year-olds who had to be potty trained and preferably attending five days a week.

Teaching had to wait. It was then I was approached by Catholic Ed to tutor a special needs student in my home. Funding had been approved for a few hours each week. The student would turn ten in nine months so until then my task was to prepare him for Special School.

It was an inspired situation. I doubt such special educational support arrangements would be allowed today with all the occupational health and safety regulations. But the strength of coming to the home was that we could use every resource, and I had plenty. There was no fear of other children rushing in and taking over. The young student's language was limited. He couldn't read and was easily overwhelmed by the slightest noise or movement.

My toddler loved him. They laughed at the same things. We'd go down to the large concrete apron of a drive out the back. I'd write the student's name in huge letters in coloured chalk. We'd walk around each letter sounding it out as we walked and talked and laughed.

By the end of the lesson, it was the toddler who knew the letters while M was still uncertain. Over time, the macro letters gradually diminished until they could be written on a card. That was how we built up a reading vocabulary: Mummy, Daddy. M was so excited. It was as though he'd been given keys to the universe and, in a way, he had.

He believed he was reading and that belief propelled him further than anyone expected. Each time he arrived at the front door, his smile was broader. He no longer hung back in his mother's shade.

After some months, he was old enough to go to Special School. We said our goodbyes. M was trusting with an affectionate nature. I prayed he'd always be supported and protected. For weeks, Paul kept running to the front window looking for him. To help him through the transition, we'd go down to the concrete apron and write words for M. We'd write the words with chalk. Then we started writing big words and cards and soon the budding reader had words of his own.

I missed the stimulation of the tutoring and told my friend, Val, when she called in to say hello. She kept me up-to-date with staff and work.

She told me how much she enjoyed her part-time uni studies. She'd enrolled in English 101.

Val had become one of those significant people in my life. She was old enough to be my mother. She was a good soul, who wanted to be a mother herself and would've made a wonderful one but, unfortunately, it never happened. I'll always remember a particular conversation we had not long after we met. It seeded our friendship. It was when we were sitting in the tiny staffroom at St P's. I announced we planned to start a family in the new year.

'You mean to say you hope.'

'Yes.'

'You can't assume you will.'

Why was she challenging me?

Val shrugged, tilted her head. 'Just saying. Things don't always turn out the way you expect.'

I was taken aback by her forthrightness but she was right. I knew she was right because I'd been trying to fall pregnant and it hadn't happened. There was something crystal-clear about Val. She always spoke to the truth. I liked that.

When she called in another afternoon after school, she talked more about her studies. I admitted I suffered from brain hunger. She suggested I enrol. 'Start small – try one unit.'

It was 1976. Our son was two years old and Gough Whitlam had introduced free university, which meant it would be possible. Mature-age women and working-class men were flocking to uni. It was no surprise when fourteen years later, privileged white-collared politicians stopped free tertiary education saying it was only youth from wealthy families who benefited. I'm sure they did benefit but it wasn't the whole picture.

When fees were re-introduced, it was, in my experience, while attending a university in a working-class town, the women and working-class men who suffered from the re-introduction of fees. So many of them had to drop their studies once fees were re-introduced.

Women already found it hard to make ends meet on the small budget on which we had to live. It was accepted practice in our circle of family and friends that a stay-at-home mum be given a budget for housekeeping on a fortnightly basis. After all, she was the mere worker bee.

Thomas more often than not came with me to do the fortnightly shop. That way, no money changed hands. That was the downside but there was an upside. I was always relieved when he was there physically to juggle a full shopping trolley and keep watch on an active young child while carrying things up the steep back stairs. The physicality of caring for a young child was full-time and demanding. I often smiled at the term 'the weaker sex.' Who was the weaker sex? I couldn't see one.

It was raining one morning, so a group of mothers gathered at my place for morning tea. Our children could play in our indoor/outdoor room. One of the neighbours happened to mention that when she was making the bed that morning, she discovered more money than usual left under the pillow. She giggled.

Who was going to ask her what she was talking about? Was it her birthday? What did she mean, more than usual?

She looked confused. 'Aren't you given cash for (pause) intimacy?'

The room stopped breathing.

Someone asked, 'How do you feel about that?'

'I hate it but it means I have spending money. Otherwise, how do you-?'

It was 1976, years after Germaine Greer's claim in *The Female Eunuch* that marriage was a form of prostitution which at the time I thought was pure hyperbole but here was a neighbour, a married woman, sitting in my living room, telling us how she was paid for 'intimacy,' as she called it. More troubling, was the fact that she believed it was common practice.

Until this time, before I moved north, I'd moved in very private circles where you kept everything to yourself. At that time, we were very much a Christian society, living by church and state laws and customs without any thought for women. Romantic love and motherly love were expected to be infinite and non-exhaustive. The martyr's mat and doormat were both sides of the same Home Sweet Home coiled mat found on every front door threshold.

Did my neighbour's husband realise he demeaned his wife?

Our group was made up of nurse, speech therapist, teacher, secretary, librarian. We often laughed out of sheer frustration but, in this instance, it was our silence that shrieked. How best to answer?

It was uncomfortable and shocking, so we came at it sideways.

Everyone agreed it was difficult lassooing our financier into a shopping centre. We agreed how demeaning it was to plead for more money for food or clothing and how frustrating it was when we had to explain that a child had grown out of their shoes and needed the next size. We agreed it was hard going to bed with the accountant.

If only her husband had paid her for every meal she cooked. If he'd paid her for every load of washing she hung out, brought in, folded, ironed, put away. If he'd paid her for every time she made the beds, changed the linen, cleaned the bathroom, scraped the detritus off the toilet bowl and vacuumed dead cells. It seemed her work as full-time wife and mother had no value.

We decided there and then that we'd happily take over the family budget, pay bills, mow lawns, maintain gardens a fraction of the week while our better halves took full responsibility for the children's emotional, practical and domestic needs; without pay, of course.

And he'd have to ask for money nicely and give a full account of how he intended to spend it. When he came home, he needed to hand her the dockets. He could keep the change. We only included that one because one of the group's husbands expected that of her.

Our neighbour had opened up a lively discussion which lasted weeks. We'd all worked full-time before becoming full-time mums, some of us in leadership positions, some in-charge of company budgets; some trained staff, some were in charge of lives. We understood the pressures and politics of full-time work but nothing prepared us for the loss of dignity, and dismissiveness of our personhood, when we became a full-time mothers at home.

One of the group was indignant that her husband insisted on choosing her swimmers. Jill preferred a trim one-piece swimsuit, dark in colour, to protect her four-child-bearing stomach. She deplored the skimpiness of the brightly coloured suggestion of a bikini her husband would choose. She had to parade before him while he made up his mind. His choice always required her to shave herself until she looked and felt like a plucked chicken. He believed he had the final say because he was the one who paid.

Laughter was our safety valve. None of us ever expected the institution of marriage to condone such indignities. Our mothers had never said a word. Here we compensated by laughing uproariously. Our primal screams diffused the next and the next disclosed indignity.

Had I continued with paid work, I would never have learnt about this underbelly. Currents of change enabled our generation to speak out. Education and access to childcare caused rips in the traditional fabric, revealing so many open wounds.

The wounds weren't anyone's fault. They were social, cultural, political wounds and they needed to be addressed. While sharing made us stronger, calmer, kinder, we didn't share our dirty laundry – not really, not the real nitty-gritty of what went on behind closed doors, not intentionally, anyway.

# Guilty Pleasure

I followed up V's suggestion and enrolled in one unit of English for next semester. On my first night, I had to find a small room where a tutorial was being held. Guilty pleasure powered my step as I walked along the gum-lined path. There was fragrance of eucalypt and trill of birdsong. Fortunately, gravity was at work for if sheer bliss had wings, I would've been up there in the clouds.

Senses overload; each leaf singing. Someone had cared enough to landscape this bland, newish brick building in such a way that trees and birds were stars on Mother Nature's stage. It was equal to a rush of excitement; an opening of the heart; gushes of fresh raw energy; a butterfly taking deep breaths as it crawled out of its chrysalis.

Apart from beautiful beaches in this coal town, the setting of the university on Awabakal country seemed like a genuine attempt at reconciliation, at a time when reconciliation was but a mere bulb. The university itself was one of beauty in stark contrast to a dark energy which had seeped into the coal seams of this town.

While there were areas of bleakness, the people wore a distinctive pride. Besides, if you didn't like it, you could leave. They wouldn't stop you. They didn't need you. What was keeping you? I'd wished a formidable Novacastrian would shirt-front me and tell me to leave, give me a reason to run, but strolling through the university there was a grounding. My skin tingled with hope, my gut did backflips.

Two days before this evening, I'd walked the grounds hand in hand with my chatty toddler. I needed to get a sense of place; needed to find the library, which was built snugly into the landscape. I organised a library card and paid union dues. Paul and I found a sleek canteen. I picked up a tray and we moved along the line. We oohed and aahed at the choice; chose our sandwiches and drinks then sat at a big table in a crowded buzz.

Soon we followed students as they strolled to lectures. We crossed creeks on footbridges shaded by tall eucalypts. Everything about the sympathetic beauty of this place made me feel like I'd come home. Hopefully, I'd quench my unquenchable thirst and learn what is and what isn't and maybe understand more about the scheme of things in life; understand more about the how, the why, the when, the where.

On my first night, I had an English tutorial to go to followed by two hours of lectures. I climbed a few steps and entered the main admin building carrying a heavy emotional backpack and an image of my young son before me, laughing with his daddy. I needed to see it. It's what I hope is happening at home. Usually at this time of night, I'd be intent on setting the table and serving dinner on time, synching with other mothers in our small valley where family sounds reverberated.

Family, friends and neighbours had wondered out loud how I could possibly be an effective play-dough provider, cleaner upperer, youth leader, chorister, committee member, painter, tutor as well as wife, mother, daughter, friend, neighbour and a student for three hours one night a week. But teaching and mothering had taught me fine-honed skills: how to prioritise and elasticise time. Some friends thought my entry into university was a rejection of the predestined homemaker's role. Some saw it as a rejection or judgment of them. It was none of that. It was about hunger. I was hungry for brain food.

As I climbed the stairs to the first floor, I steadied my uncertain gait with gratitude. Thank you, Lord, thank you, Gough; free university, undeserved privilege. I identified as a mature-age student willingly fracturing the stereotypical wife and mother image and swimming against the tide of negative feedback and diverse opinions.

There was a rush of early evening freshness; new opportunities unlocked gender doors. The changes asked a lot of men of the traditional ilk, particularly those who saw no need for change.

That first night, before I left, I'd set the dinner table and had prepared the evening meal but Thomas was less than impressed. Traditional roles were being dismantled in the crescent. In some households in our neighbourhood, fathers were known to be ironing their own shirts. One husband liked to show how progressive he was. He'd sing lustily as he hung out their fourth child's nappies on the clothesline. It caused mutterings in the crescent. How embarrassing for XY to have XX hang out nappies! Obviously, she wasn't coping, ignoring the fact that she and he were sharing to the degree there were never any angry loud voices coming from their back porch.

The husband was quite the entertainer. He liked bringing the ironing board out onto the back veranda. Our backyards all looked onto each other. As the crescent curled around, so did our yards. He had a stage of sorts. If I dared to appear in my backyard in short shorts, there'd be whistling and 'hello beautiful.'

He wouldn't have been aware that his unwanted attention changed the way I behaved and dressed. If I knew he was home, I avoided going outside. I was annoyed that I had to lock the back door should my son and I lie down for an afternoon nap. More than once, he suddenly appeared just inside my back door.

One time, he walked into the hallway which led to the main bedroom where I was dressing. His response was 'I knocked.'

'I didn't hear you.'

'... your door's unlocked.'

Most households where husbands helped out were not as demonstrative as Jack, thank heavens, but for families where husbands didn't understand the need to help, loud disagreements echoed around Happy Nappy Valley.

Gender roles in the crescent were definitely flexing but progress seemed to depend on the inner transition of the man of the house who could or couldn't understand the changes taking place in our world which were quite different to that of his father's.

Thomas, who was reared in a progressive household, held up the attractive, aproned wife portrayed in the 1950s film *Cheaper by the Dozen* with Clifton Webb and Myrna Loy as his ideal of marriage. He idealised Webb and Loy's roles. With my new-found isolation, Thomas had become more vocal about what he considered to be my wifely duties. It was a slow creep. Each minuscule wifely duty squeezed me into Adam's side. It was an uncomfortable fit but I needed to keep the peace. Meanwhile, Thomas acted on his mediaeval anointed role with increasing confidence, with full support of the church and state at his back.

In his eyes, it was simple. I had a pre-ordained female role. Sometimes, I'd question his unrealistic expectations and he'd look puzzled and hurt. Surely, I knew my place. I've been given the right to vote. I owned my own car. What more did I want?

'You're lucky to have a man to look after you.'

I wanted to ask who looked after who but I didn't. As we hurtled towards the burnt-out end of the twentieth century, my wings were already seriously singed. Our marriage had been based on the stereotypical Christian hand-holding-couple-front. Saint Paul could never have envisaged the advent of the Pill, nor the rise in women's education, nor the power play it'd bring; it's core being economics and ego.

I never gave up hope of hearing the heartbeat of our union; the gentle thrum after a meal when we could sit and talk, console and plan. I had an expectation of companionship, seeing us sitting close together at the end of day, similar to that I'd seen shared by my parents.

As I walked out of the lecture theatre and into the night air, my first thought was of home. Would Paul be asleep? Hopefully, yes. I chatted with another mature-age student as we walked to the car park. She was as thrilled as me to have such an incredible opportunity. Said she never thought it'd happen. Same here.

When I turned into our steep driveway, a wave of apprehension tipped my balance. Lamp lights flickered. As I closed the garage door and made my way up the outside stairs, I couldn't help but smile at the thought of what a momentous night it had been. There needed to be champagne and fireworks. I was full of gratitude. I looked up to the stars and knew I wasn't alone. I'd just found my home of learning, after years of longing to be in such an atmosphere. My spirit soared.

I opened the back door brimming with the past three euphoric hours. Thomas stood by the door like an usher. On second thoughts, he looked more like a security guard. I would've handed him a late note if I had one. I reached up and kissed his cheek.

'You're late.'

'I didn't finish lectures till nine.'

'It's quarter past.'

'Had to drive home.'

'That's twelve minutes.'

'Had to walk from the lecture theatre to the car.' I resented the unnecessary interrogation. 'You go out all the time. Do I time you? Am I upset when you get home?'

By that time of night, I usually would've bathed Paul and put him to bed. I'd have washed up and been sitting in my designated colonial recliner in front of the TV, in my rightful place, beside my husband in our newly decorated lime-green-on-white family room.

Thomas had wallpapered lime-green and white paisley on the kitchen and family room walls. We bought a lime vinyl-topped round table with white legs accompanied by four lime-coloured wooden chairs with lime metal legs and with floral lime and white vinyl covers. On the floor in the centre of the room was a large lime and white swirled thick rug spread out in front of the colonial floral covered recliners. Tall white bookcases stood in the family room on either side of the double glass doors which opened up into the living room.

I entered into the lime-green spirit and left my books on the side kitchen bench. I walked inside to kiss my son good night. I expected he'd be sound asleep. He was often difficult to get to sleep and when he did it was very deep. When I looked down at our beloved son, with his long eyelashes forming little smiles on his eyelids, I heard him catch his breath - again and again.

He'd been crying. For how long? I lent over and patted him rhythmically and firmly until his breathing evened out – ssshhh-ssshhh-ssshhh.

I walked into the kitchen. 'What's the matter with -?'

'He wouldn't go to sleep.'

I watched Thomas pace back and forth.

He said, 'This is not going to work, you know.'

His pacing was earlier tonight. Whenever he wound up his emotional clock, the cat knew to disappear into the living room and hide under the two seater.

It was the same pattern the following week, so I determined to organise day lectures and tutorials, which meant trying to find almost non-existent, child-minding arrangements. The alternative was to withdraw from the course. I didn't want to do that but if I had to, I had to.

Free university studies was a great opportunity and I dearly wanted to continue but, on the domestic front, Thomas's disapproval of my studies reverberated. 'None of my mates' wives are studying.'

I stopped mentioning essays or exams and kept evidence of my studies out of sight. Containing my activities like this was a familiar feeling. I'd grown up keeping most achievements to myself. It was, and continued to be, necessary to fold my spreading wings in certain company. It was a struggle to rearrange lectures and tutorials to daytime and to find suitable babysitting. At the time, I'd irregularly attended a women's Bible study group.

One of the group said, 'Have you stopped to think that it might be God's way of telling you you shouldn't be studying?'

'Yes, I have, and I think it's more a reflection of the city's reluctance to provide adequate childcare.'

We were on the waiting list at the university's soon to be open, state of the art, new Montessori Day Care Centre. I was currently swapping babysitting hours with a friend. Great hope had been placed in the flourishing new university. Hopefully, it'd stop the city's brain drain. But, as population growth teetered, professionals continued to leave. How I wished I could leave with them but my husband had found his tribe. It was up to me to create my own buzz.

# The Spire

As I feared, university unsettled and challenged me and, as I hoped, extended my world. There was no longer a straight line as guide; now so many paths. It was with some timidity I looked at my long-held beliefs and opened them up to the universe.

I began to see myself not as a separate entity or a predestined one but as part of an amazing loving whole; a miraculous, mysterious whole - all as one, whose energy was divine light and love. How exciting it'd be if we gathered in communities on Sundays to give thanks for the mysteries.

My spirit soared on currents of new thought and greater understanding. As it gained altitude, it was vertiginous; as life saving as intensive care; closer to the divine, home to the universe within; a new paradigm.

And there were a few more surprises in store. Until now, my university reading had been censored by my blinkered evangelical eyes. At uni, I read English 101 texts at a distance, not wanting to be 'of the world' and not wanting to be 'led into temptation.'

I read the set uni texts when I sat up in bed beside Thomas while he read his train magazines. I read the set texts for enjoyment first; a super fast read then again more slowly. William Golding's *The Spire* exuded beauty and passion in language and worship. Some of it was uplifting, inspirational. I was excited. I walked into the lecture theatre expecting to reach heights of wisdom and knowledge.

The lecturer stumbled a little as he walked to the podium. I'd never met him before. I assumed he'd had a stroke or suffered from cerebral palsy or maybe he'd had polio when young. But no. His slurred speech cancelled out any sympathy. It was the case of an highly inebriated one delivering a lecture focusing on black magic and the phallic symbol. I sat through the lecture feeling uncomfortable and ignorant.

Walking to the car park after lectures, I said to my new friend that I knew nothing about black magic and had never heard of a phallic symbol. Was it something religious? She was very polite when she explained. I don't know how she didn't laugh because, once she told me, I couldn't stop.

After that, I saw them everywhere. How could I look at the spire on a cathedral ever again without seeing an ambitious, wilful, erect penis blocking the more aspirational heavenly directed prayers? If this was deep and meaningful literary critical analysis, I hoped there weren't going to be too many more surprises. All I could see now were overblown egos and f-you-all buildings everywhere.

If indeed the erection of the spire in Golding's world was built without solid foundations, that would be magic of a kind, but it also meant ruthlessness and a strong will on a grandiose scale. If faith was strong, it could move mountains; Matthew 17:20.

My mind was moving mountains. There was another whole realm of interpretation which opened up perspectives; masculine and feminine everywhere. How could I come back from this? Nothing would ever be the same. There was an unsteadiness in my tread. I was stunned that between the lines language could be so powerful and could expand the physicality and volume of my world.

Historically, the church and its spire, once the highest building in town, shared a relationship with business and, soon, business buildings were the tallest. Where were the feminine buildings? The Opera House, perhaps, with its drapery of sails. The feminine was obvious in Nature with its pert breasts and taut thighs; the harbour as womb. I'd always seen that.

As my friend and I reached the dimly lit car park, I saw cars in a new light. There were feminine and masculine cars everywhere. I consciously unlocked my very feminine, burgundy Renault 10 and drove out onto the main road with its very masculine street poles.

*The Spire* – mountains moved – to God be the glory. I could see I needed to reread it. Did I agree with the lecturer's interpretation? That really didn't matter. The protagonist was a man filled with misguided faith and passion. He believed that the spire could stand without a firm foundation. He didn't see it for what it was, a stubborn vision; a case of ruthless passion which almost cost one man his life. The cleric's ego ran away with itself just as our lecturer had run away with the bottle. I'd have to be careful. Could all this learning become a ruthless passion? Could I get drunk on it?

One day as I hurried towards a tutorial, my inner smile was joy. I'd just left my son safely ensconced in the new uni daycare centre. I was alert to light and shade tangoing on the path and thought, that's me dancing, when, suddenly, I saw perched on the top of a small recently painted white pole, highlighted by the sun, a possum; a beautiful possum.

I stopped. Our eyes met. Eyes held eyes. It was a significant exchange. I smiled at our mutual trust. While we both might have seemed out of place, we shared something in common. In spite of everything, we delighted in just being there, in the sunshine, in that exulted moment.

I was out of touch writing essays. My essay results always disappointed and mystified me. They never matched tutorial grades. Being ignorant that a student was expected to rely solely on recognised reliable sources, and not use my own thoughts, I blithely went ahead using one or two sources but always had the audacity to offer my own, not realising that an undergraduate's thoughts had no value.

I thought uni was all about exploring and learning how to think. Over time, one or two tutors, who were post graduate students, asked for permission to quote some of my tutorial content for their own research. I was chuffed but had no idea that meant I had something of value to say.

My close knowledge of the Scriptures helped me. Having grown up in a world steeped in metaphor, symbolism and the beautiful King James language, I'd unknowingly stored within me a rich treasure. Even so, my essays were only ever pass.

One day when I went to pick up an essay, the head of the English Department saw me standing at the front desk.

She walked out of her office as I glanced at my low pass mark. She said, 'What do you think?'

'Disappointed.'

The mark indicated a poor effort but I'd spent hours on it. It was a buzz. I'd enjoyed uncovering the layers of meaning. Metaphors vibrated between lines. I'd held them up to the light; examined their literary veins which flowed with emotion and meaning. This particular essay involved some Dylan Thomas poem. It had so many reverberations it was dizzying. I used two sources for research but couldn't find a source that supported my own ideas. Even so, I naïvely put them into the essay.

The English Head offered a suggestion. 'We have a visiting Canadian professor here. I gave her some essays to mark and yours was one of them. Would you like to discuss it with her?'

'Thank you, but not really.'

Me in discussion with a professor? I shuddered at the thought.

When I walked into her small room, I saw dust motes floated between us in the warm rays of afternoon light. The professor indicated where I should sit. She was tall, blondish, wearing a bright shoulder-padded red blazer with large gold buttons. All I could see before me was bright red and gold professorial power.

She smiled and said, 'It was a good essay but the reason you got such a poor mark is you didn't credit your sources. You have to credit your sources.'

'I thought I did.'

'No, you didn't. For example...'

And she quoted one of my thoughts, one I'd had while sitting on the back step. I'd been dreaming its meaning while staring at the curly willow. I rarely had quiet times like that, unless I got up very early of a morning but, in this instance, I'd grabbed the opportunity to work on the assignment when my son was invited to play next door with his little mate. I could hear them racing their tot rods down the steep slope of the driveway. They were yelling; breaking a sound barrier of sorts. It was a happy sound and I wasn't directly responsible; momentary freedom.

It was hard to explain my process of thought and how I arrived at this particular idea. It had been difficult expressing it in simple terms on paper.

'Oh,' I said, 'I thought that because...'

'Yes, but you have to acknowledge who gave you the idea. You must've read it somewhere.'

'No - no-one gave it to me.'

If I could've sat her down beside me on the top step that afternoon, she might've come to the same conclusion.

The professor proceeded to list more examples, all of which were my own. Each time, I explained.

Finally, she said, 'I believe you. Now, knock over your degree as fast as you can. Do your Masters then get on with your PhD. This is PhD material.'

A PhD in English? I didn't know I could get one. And why would I need one? I already had teaching qualifications. An acquaintance of mine had a PhD but he was an engineer. I'd assumed PhD's had something to do with engineering.

'For your essays, remember we can't accept your thoughts.'

From the gut I shot, 'But how can I retain my intellectual integrity if I spend years regurgitating other people's material?'

She sat upright in her chair, looked me in the eye and said, 'I managed to retain mine.'

The power base sitting opposite me didn't realise she'd burst a balloon and when it burst it stung. I needed to explain. I didn't mean to sound smart-assish but I must've because as I spoke, the professor's neck and cheeks turned the colour of her blazer.

'Does that mean I can't use my own interpretation?'

'That's right. Not at undergraduate level unless you can back it up with a recognised source.'

In spite of my unintended impertinence, the professor was fair. She said she believed the work was mine but she wouldn't be giving me a better mark because she couldn't. I wasn't a recognised source and I should remember that when writing my next essay.think?'

'Keep it. The time will come when one day you can use it.'

As she talked, a strong image of our large backyard, with its seven neighbours, came to mind. While I belonged sitting here on this chair at one level, and I belonged sitting out the back watching children play on another level, I felt fenced in on both levels. In an instant, I knew I'd not be returning next year. I'd almost completed the extra four units I needed to upgrade my teaching qualifications.

I would enrol years later after a friend told me about a new unit – Creative Writing and Dramatic Prose – a blank page on which to write – that definitely sounded more like me.

# Weak Ankles

We'd been in Newcastle seven years. Thomas made it clear that he didn't want to go back to Sydney. The compromise was to invest in a more substantial home. We bought a beautiful architect-designed home at Highfields. It overlooked the bush and out to Glenrock Lagoon and the Pacific Ocean.

From the minute we settled into the new house, it demanded my attention, so one day I stood in the expansive hallway and spoke to it in a no-nonsense tone. I needed to curb its attitude. 'Yes, I think you're beautiful and we'll be happy together but I'm not going to be your slave. You're a home – not a show pony.'

Things went quiet after that.

The backyard was like most backyards where children run free and discover make-believe worlds, be it Narnia or a treehouse in the old turpentine tree in the back corner of the yard or in the earnestly built cages by Paul and his young builder friends. They built a large cage for the duck and the old wardrobe was turned onto its back and sectioned off into apartments for the guinea pigs.

Two miscarriages had made me super-appreciative of our young son's vibrant life. Energy-wise and capacity-wise, he was equal to six. Responsibilities kept him and his friends fully occupied looking after the animals, feeding and cleaning out cages or preparing emergency cages out of discarded fish tanks stored in the young herpetologist's bedroom. The boys also cared for injured reptiles or mammals they found on their Glenrock Lagoon excursions.

As a family, we were rich in friendship and there was always something to look forward to. On Sundays, we sang in the choir. Worship inspired and fed the spirit. Choir performances at Christmas and Easter were always busy times.

I'd recently read an article about a childhood hero, Betty Cuthbert, who'd been diagnosed with multiple sclerosis. I had symptoms which sounded frighteningly similar. It was enough to slow me down. I spoke to Thomas about it. I discussed with him some of the changes I needed to make, with the hope my health would improve.

One of the changes was to stop choral work. As much as I loved singing and enjoyed the fellowship, I no longer wanted to sing sustained high notes. At times, after a long singing practice or performance, I experienced loss of power that night and the next day.

When we were due to go to the next choir practice, I said to Thomas, 'I won't go tonight. I'm too tired. Will you give my apologies?'

'I'm not going without you.'

'That's up to you.'

'No. It's up to you. If we don't go, it isn't fair on the others.'

'I'm not stopping you. It's my body that's stopping me. It's hard to explain.'

I'd been minimising warning signs that something was seriously wrong for months now. Vertigo attacks followed intermittent loss of strength on the left side and they were becoming more frequent. I ignored the increase of ridiculously painful migraines, the worst ones being relieved by putting a tiny dissolvable pill under my tongue. I put it all down to personal stress, well aware of the strain that years of stored stress can have on areas of weakness in the body.

I'd recently withdrawn from university studies due to intermittent loss of strength, and the feeling that when I walked I was out of alignment. I'd stopped tutoring. But even with a change of pace, there was no difference. I wanted to yell, 'Stop the world – I need a break – I need to get off – now.'

After a particularly nasty vertigo attack, my doctor referred me to a specialist whose rooms resembled a wombat's burrow.

He looked into my eyes with some sophisticated-looking machinery and said, 'Let's sit down – I have a few questions.' He picked up a pen. 'I can see from your eyes you didn't have polio when you were a child, but you had something. What was it? Do you know?'

'My mother said I had weak ankles.'

'No. It's not that. Ask her again. There's something more as to why you wore irons.'

'She said it was borderline.'

'Borderline what?'

'I don't know. She said she couldn't remember.'

'Ask her again.'

During each vertigo attack, I felt like I was hurtling through space, spinning every which way. While it appeared to be an eternity of black on black, there were stars. Everything spun faster than my imagination. I couldn't look up or down. No fixed sight. If I tried to open my eyes it brought on projectile vomiting. After an attack, my left side would stubbornly steer to one side for days. I was in need of Bob Jane T-Mart's wheel alignment.

I was thirty-seven, busy-busy. I'd regained my weight but with each kilo there were louder thunder claps in my head. Clusters of migraines rolled in and out, one after the other, the last time for four months, the longest time ever.

The night I took the first blood pressure tablet, I fell into a sound sleep. I stirred in the early morning and tried to turn over but couldn't. I assumed it must've been a side effect from the new tablet, so I drifted back to sleep.

The day before, I'd been to see the diagnostic physician for a routine check-up. He was pleased that my weight issue had been resolved. The effects of my fast metabolic rate were now understood. It had taken twelve months of concentrated effort to regain weight, but the riddle of vertigo hadn't been solved.

The physician was particularly concerned about my rising blood pressure. 'Your blood pressure's been too high for too long.'

The GP had noted that, too. He believed it was directly related to my home situation. 'You're not in a very good situation... have you ever thought about leaving?'

I was shocked when he first said that. He'd been our family GP since we first moved to Newcastle; a fifteen-year family history which I imagined would have its own subtext. But, what did he know that I didn't?

As I sat in the chair, I looked past the doctor to the faithful old camellia outside the window. It had survived heatwaves, blustery winds and storms. I thought, oh, to be as brave and as resilient as that!

I blurted out, 'I'm afraid of how he might react if I tried to leave.' I couldn't believe I'd said it. It felt so disloyal.

The GP leaned in on his desk and said in a firm but gentle voice, 'I'd give it some thought if I were you. If you want to talk to someone about it, I can refer you to –'

'Yes, I'd like to talk to someone.'

Next morning, I sat at the painting table as usual. I faced the southern window – good light and no shadows. It was overcast so unusually glarey. I tilted the venetian blind to cut out the glare. I was doing very fine raised paste work on china. While I painted I liked to listen to the radio but, suddenly, I felt disconnected, totally disconnected.

I jumped up, a flight response, and headed for the kitchen. My heart pounded. What was happening? I reassured myself that I was okay but I knew I wasn't. Was this what they called a panic attack? I shook. Made a cup of hot Milo and tried to walk back down the hallway. It seemed so much longer than usual. The floor seemed to suck up every soft, rubbery step I took. Would I ever reach the end? It felt like I was caught in quicksand.

As I sat at the painting table, sipping milk, I looked out the window to distract myself. I took in the tree fern's line. It was an elegant line. I finished my milo and picked up my brush and started to apply raised paste to a small cartouche. It was on a demonstration piece for a course I was running - showing students how to make raised paste from powder. Later we were to gild it with unburnished gold, fire, then burnish it, with gloves on, while handling the small stick of fine fibreglass.

I had no memory of the rest of the day.

After cooking the evening meal, I called, 'Dinner's ready.'

I turned to carry the plates across to the table but my left leg wouldn't move. I tried again. It ignored me. I put the plates down and put my hands on my hips, puzzled. My left hip felt different. There were pins and needles running along sections of my left side. I tested the right side. All good. It knew exactly what to do. The numbness on my left side spread up and down at the same pace as my panic.

I said to Paul, 'Get your father, quick – please. Quick.'

I tried to reach for the phone but couldn't move.

Thomas called back, 'I'm watching the news.'

I yelled back, 'I'm the news right now. Quick – ring the doctor.'

It was after hours. In hindsight, we should've called an ambulance but who would've thought it was serious if there was no pain? They were pins and needles going crazy on my left side but there was no pain, so I assumed it couldn't be too serious.

The call centre operator asked Thomas, 'Is she in pain?'

'No.'

While we waited for someone to come, my darling son raced in to his bedroom, got Big Ted off his bed and he and Big Ted hopped up into bed with me and they never left my side. Their body contact and warmth settled me.

After an hour's wait, I asked Thomas to ring the after hours number again.

'This time, say I'm in pain.'

Soon a young locum arrived and examined me. 'You need to go to hospital...'

Out of earshot, the doctor told Thomas he believed I'd had a cerebrovascular accident (CVA). 'I can ring an ambulance for you or –'

Thomas said, 'No, I'll take her.'

Paul stayed at a neighbour's place overnight and it was with some difficulty that I lent on Thomas and made my way down the internal stairs to the garage. It was as if my left side had stayed on the bed.

When we arrived at the hospital, my left hand seemed oblivious to what was expected. When someone held a pen out for me to sign the admission form my left hand didn't know what to do. My right hand signed it instead. There seemed to be no memory of my left side. It was like it didn't exist, but I knew it was there, because I could see it. I couldn't feel or communicate with it at but, judging by the careful and controlled actions of nursing staff, I knew something had to be seriously wrong with it.

While we waited for a neurologist to come, Thomas paced the small room.

I said, 'Why don't you sit down?'

He couldn't sit. He kept pacing the small room. With no neurologist in sight, Thomas kissed me.

I mistook the kiss for a spontaneous sign of concern, for me being in this situation. I smiled and said, 'That's nice. I needed that.'

'I'd better get a move on, sweetheart.'

'What do you mean?'

'I've got work tomorrow.'

I was speechless. He was saying goodbye – not I love you – I'm here with you – I won't leave you. Don't worry, sweetheart, I have your back.

I held up my good hand. 'Don't go. Not yet. Can't you take tomorrow off? We don't know what's happening.' I needed Thomas to sit beside me, talk to me, preferably hold my hand and distract me. Talk about anything – even trains. I needed to be distracted from my frozen fear because I was aware of the paralysis creeping towards my neck.

Thomas walked to the door. 'Sweetheart, you'll be right.'

'Work will understand if you can't go in.'

He hovered in the doorway. 'I'm in the middle of a big roster.'

'Surely, others can help.'

'There's nothing to worry about. You'll be fine. I'd better go.'

He smiled. I didn't. I couldn't believe he was leaving me with an obviously serious undiagnosed medical condition. Whatever his hidden agenda was these days, it had a hold of him. I could see clearly now that whatever it was, he considered it more important than me.

He said, 'Sweetheart, make sure you rest.'

I wanted to scream – if you really look at me, you'll see I'm not going anywhere. Even my speech had slowed. To say I was hurt at his lack of compassion was an understatement. I was shocked. I didn't even watch the back of him walk away.

After Thomas left, an overwhelming quiet filled the room. I stared at a small painting hanging on the wall. It was across the room from my bed; a nondescript sanguine landscape which held my attention while I waited. I listened to noises in the hallway, hoping to hear a doctor's footsteps coming my way.

The room seemed ultra-quiet but it was then I realised it wasn't the room that was quiet – it was my head. It was so quiet I wondered if this was how death arrived? Nurses kept coming in and out taking obs and being so kind. Did death just creep in unannounced without bothering to check in at the front desk? If so, there'd definitely be no raging 'against the dying of the light.' I silently feared I was slipping into 'that good night.'

The neurologist arrived very late. Dr. T and I recognised each other. We sang in the same small acappella group.

He looked around. 'Is Thomas here?'

I shook my head.

'I thought he might –'

'He was but he had to go.'

'I'm sorry you had to wait so long. Now – if I'm correct, you have a history of migraine.'

'Yes, and the past few months they've been terrible. I haven't been able to turn my head.'

'Are you in pain now?'

'No. My head's gone really quiet, which is really unusual.'

'There's nothing for you to worry about... paralysis is temporary. You can get it from migraine.'

'I didn't know that. That's a relief. Can I go home?'

'Not so fast. If it's a migraine, you'll be home soon but I'd like to keep an eye on you just to be on the safe side.'

Next morning, Dr T and a junior neurologist conducted some tests. While Dr. T. seemed happy with the results, the subtle frown on the junior neurologist's face said otherwise.

He said, 'The response in the left eye –'

Dr. T leant in. He lifted the eyelid and – 'Mmm. I concur. A CT scan might be necessary – no hurry. We'll pop her in for Monday.'

It was Friday and I stayed in a very noisy, busy emergency ward until Monday. Instructions to Sister were that I was to stay in bed. If I wanted to go to the loo, a wheelchair and assistance would be necessary. These precautions were to be undertaken until the results of the CT scan came through.

Dr. T turned to me and said, 'Don't worry. I'm confident you'll be out of here well before then.'

I needed to believe him, but I was the only who knew that the paralysis was still stealing more of my side.

After they left, a patient in the bed opposite, climbed out of bed and hurried over. She pulled up the chair next to me and said, 'What's happening?'

She would've heard every word because the ward went extra quiet whenever doctors arrived. We'd listen to one another's diagnoses filter through partly drawn curtains.

'I'm having a CT scan on Monday but I might be out of here before then. He thinks it's a migraine.'

The retired matron leant forward in the chair and whispered, 'I think you've had a stroke but I'm not a doctor.'

That put up my heart rate. She had to be wrong. I couldn't have had a stroke. I'd seen lots of stroke patients in the years we visited my great grandmother in the nursing home. Stroke victims were old. I was thirty-seven.

I didn't see my neurologist friend again until after the scan. The resident neurologist and his assistant continued to conduct tests. They knew, and I knew, there'd been a deterioration. While there was no pain, the paralysis had set in from my neck down to my feet. The pins and needles had gone. Everything was silent – nothing. Sometimes, I was surprised when I looked down and saw my left arm or leg. I'd forgotten all about them. I kept touching them to remind myself they were there.

My matron friend was moved out of emergency and admitted to a ward. She'd been a marvellous support and I was sorry to see her go. I stayed in emergency with two men: a middle-aged Englishman who was kind and funny and the other man, about the same age as him, made constant demands of the nursing staff. He shared his anger with us for two nights, calling out in the loudest voice to whoever would listen.' I want to die. I'm dying. Nurse? Where are you? Nurse? Are you going to let me die on my own?'

I couldn't very well call out 'shut up' to a dying man.

During the day, he was quiet and slept. At night, he came alive. On the third night, staff took pity on us and moved him into a room of his own. Finally, we got a decent sleep, at least, as decent as anyone can get in an emergency department.

# CVA

Monday morning. CT scan.

Soon someone from admin came in and said, 'Let me help you with these admission forms.'

'Am I being admitted?'

'Yes.'

Next thing, Sister bustled in and said, 'You're a lucky girl. You're going upstairs. It'll be quieter up there.'

Fortuitously, I was moved into the same ward as my matron friend from Emergency. Once again, I was in the bed opposite her.

Around midday, Dr T appeared at the doorway accompanied by two assistants. He held his hands together, praying-mantis-style, as if he was about to bow and ask for forgiveness.

I felt his discomfort so spoke first. "I don't like the look of this.'

'I'm so sorry, Anne. You've had a cerebral haemorrhage.'

'A ce-re-what?'

'A cerebral haemorrhage, a bleed in the brain.'

'Is that a stroke?'

'Yes. I'm so sorry. I owe you an apology. It was your history of migraine that –'

By now, I was completely paralysed down the left side, from my toes up to my chin. I could put a pin in the middle of my chest and find the micrometer between numbness and feeling. I could talk but words came slowly while some disappeared for some time. Some I didn't find until years later. If more than one person spoke at a time, it sounded like a racket.

Dr. T said, 'You've got youth on your side and your veins are in very good condition. That's what's saved you.'

'Do you think the new blood pressure tablets might've –?'

'No. You were lucky to be on them. It'll be months now before we know what's caused it. We'll have to wait for the blood clot to dissolve. It's difficult to see that part of the brain stem.'

'What happens now?'

'We've had a meeting and we've decided you're too young to go to a convalescent home. It'd be detrimental. You can go home in a week or two with provisos – when you're independent enough to go to and from the bathroom...'

I was relieved I could go home. While in 1981 there was no rehabilitation unit for someone my age, the neurologist gave me a marvellous goal. Who'd have thought that getting to and from the loo would one day become the sole purpose of my day and would give me a ticket to freedom? In truth, I was scared stiff. I had to make jokes about it or else I'd cry. How could this have happened? For heaven's sake, I was thirty-seven with a seven year old child, in the prime of my life.

Later that afternoon, another patient was moved into our ward. She'd been playing Pennants golf earlier in the day and suffered a major stroke. It was going to be a tough recovery for her and she'd need every bit of competitive spirit to overcome the major obstacles on her next green.

The elderly patient on my right was happily packing. 'I'm going home in the morning,' she said.

It was a surprise when in the early hours curtains were drawn and I heard nurses gently calling her name. Soon there was a quiet busyness around her. We were in the dress circle of Life and Death. It was peaceful; the staff's response reverential. This wasn't the first time someone had died in a hospital bed next to me.

When I was twelve years old, in the children's ward at the Mater Misceracordia Hospital, Wollstonecraft, my younger sister, Wendy, and I were having the same operation on the same day because we kept reinfecting each other with tonsillitis. The young girl in the bed next to me was about eight years old. Her arms and parts of her body were heavily bandaged. When the nurses came, they'd draw the curtains to do things with the little girl's bandages and she'd scream and scream.

The nurses would try and soothe her. 'It's all right, darling.'

Her screams were beyond any help. They'd draw back the curtains when they'd finished and the little girl would look across at me and whimper.

She'd cry, 'Mummy, Mummy. I want Mummy, Daddy.' And she sobbed.

A nurse would come over and say, 'It'll be visiting hours soon – Mummy'll be here soon.'

One night, the little girl, who'd been whimpering all day, especially after our parents left after visiting hours, stopped whimpering. It was after lights out and soon nurses and doctors gathered near my bed with torchlights flashing. They drew the little girl's curtains and stood whispering.

At some stage, her parents arrived. Then there was crying, broken-hearted crying. It broke my heart, too, and to this day it still breaks it. I stayed very still, hardly game enough to move or breathe. Whatever was happening behind those curtains was serious.

A nurse came and checked on me. She could see I was staring at the torchlights behind the curtains. She said, 'Everything's all right. You roll over and go to sleep.'

I must've fallen asleep because in the morning the little girl's bed was empty. I wanted to shout stop when I saw them disinfecting the bed. Soon, the bed had fresh sheets. It didn't seem right. We couldn't forget the little girl.

I saw nurses hugging and comforting each other and some of them cried. I wanted to cry, too. I knew by then that the little girl must've died and I didn't want to forget her. Nurses came and tried to cheer me up.

One nurse said, 'Why don't you get your sister and take her around the ward? Some of these children can't get out of bed. They'd love someone to talk to.'

I took Wendy to different children in the ward and we said hello. There didn't seem to be much more to say than that. I was more conscious of the little girl who was no longer crying. She seemed to be walking beside me. In my imagination, she wore a pretty blue dress.

Then I saw Mummy walk into the ward. She smiled and held out her arms. I was confused. It was too early for visiting hours.

She said, 'C'mon, help me pack your bags. You're going home.'

'Now?'

'Yes. You've been such good girls, you've got an early mark.'

Daddy was in his lunch break and he waited outside the front door of the hospital with the car motor running.

On the way home, I couldn't get the little girl out of my mind. She had to be somewhere. I asked my parents, 'Where has she gone? Not her body – where has she –the person of she gone?'

I'd never forgotten the little girl and here I was again in a hospital bed wondering where my neighbour's person had gone. Was she the overwhelming peace that flooded the ward in the quiet of the night? As we lay in our beds, could she hear our prayers for her soul, for her family, for her speedy journey home?

Death was very much on my mind in the next few days. The staff were so attentive I wondered if they expected one of us to die, too.

When it was time for me to go home, Dr T said, 'You can't be too careful.' He gave me a list of do's and don'ts and reiterated, 'Remember the next twelve months are crucial.'

He needn't have worried. Sometime during the night, I'd been given a gift; a calm certainty. No one else could see the vague image I saw in my mind of someone in a bed in a ward and I'd heard the words, 'You'll get well, get well, get well.' The words were intended for me and they were spoken so clearly and directly that my first reaction was to turn to the left to see who was speaking. Only then did I realise the voice and image had come from within.

Before I left hospital, the physiotherapist gave me my rehabilitation program. 'When your strong enough, see if you can get someone to take you to a hydrotherapy pool – preferably twice a week for twelve months... hold onto the pool's edge and walk up and down.

Start with five minutes then gradually increase it, in small increments, say to ten minutes.'

I was so thankful I could go home – some wouldn't be so lucky. Margaret, my roommate, was waiting to be taken to Hornsby, where there was a vacancy in a new rehabilitation unit, Mount Wilga.

Rehabilitation for me consisted of sleeping for two two-hour sessions twice a day. At other times, I sat in my favourite armchair in the sitting room and looked out over the trees to the ocean and counted my blessings. Light and colours and cloudscapes changed. I sensed that landforms within me were changing, too. These next steps were up to me. I didn't know what these new landforms would be like, but whatever they were like it was up to me to find out.

I'd spent years blinkering my way through much of my life. Now that functional enjoyable parts had been stripped away, and my rose-coloured glasses smashed, I found myself sitting without blinkers.

The first few weeks at home were harsh. There was anger, frustration and grief when I couldn't do the simplest thing, such as, getting my son's lunch ready for school. Thomas went to work every day. It was hard being at home on my own. I was unable to walk very far and I could only use one hand, whereas in hospital I'd been used to support and I missed the congeniality of my roommates. At home, most of the day, it was just me-and-myself looking after me.

Not having someone around during the day forced me to become independent more quickly but I had concerns. I couldn't swallow properly. Water and food ran around in my mouth. I'd lose touch with where it was. I'd cough and splutter and think I was going to choke and I worried there'd be no one there to save me. I didn't know that the left side of my tongue had been affected and from that time on I'd have trouble swallowing.

I remember telling a GP once, 'I have a drinking problem.'

She sat very still and looked deeply concerned as she repeated what I'd just said, 'You have a drinking problem.'

That's when I saw the humour in the misunderstanding. 'Oh,' I said, 'I mean I have a - ' and pointed to my throat.

The doctor said, 'A swallowing problem? Do you mean a swallowing problem?'

'Yes,' and we both laughed.

Six weeks after the CVA, I had a gastroscopy followed by weeks of Gastrogel and Dexsal. My stomach had boiled fear and screamed such outrageous obscenities that my stomach behaved as if it was an ulcer – an inner metaphor for the indignation I was feeling.

In the very early days of recovery, the world shrank to the confines of the bedroom, living room and sunroom. The telephone was part of that world too. Because we didn't live near family, I appreciated my parents' and friends' phone calls and visitors. I looked forward to my parents coming up of a weekend. They were both in their mid-sixties and still worked full-time. I worried that my CVA condition had stressed them, and I worried they were doing too much, but their love and care, and that of my young son and dear friends, were an essential part of my recovery.

From the main living room, I looked out through a large window which framed Glenrock Lagoon, meandering its way to the ocean. The ocean defined the horizon, where coal tankers queued against the skyline. I looked out over the rooftops of houses across the road, set on the low side of the street, and looked over crowns of trees of the State Conservation Reserve, a National Park.

In the silence of my distressed-how-did-I-get-here state, I began to sip on the beauty of the wide band of steely blue shantung that was the Pacific. I watched clouds form. They reminded me of times when I'd taught students about clouds; when I'd drawn a set of large cards identifying the different types. It was because of Dad's love of cloudscapes that I'd learnt to love them, too. Often, as a child, I'd find him standing in the yard smoking a cigarette and looking up at the sky.

I'd say, 'What are you looking at?'

'The clouds.'

'Why are you looking at clouds?'

'They're beautiful. They keep changing.'

I'd stand and look at them and Dad would say, 'What can you see?'

We'd have a lovely discussion about clouds and how they drew pictures and how they told us about the weather and what was to come.

I was known to be a chatterbox, so Dad would say, 'To look at clouds properly, you have to stand very still and be as quiet as them.'

# Step by Step

My parents sacrificed so much during this time. They'd travel up every second or third weekend after working five days a week. I felt so guilty. I wanted to cry. The stroke had cracked open all my emotions. I should've been looking after my parents instead of them looking after me. I should've been looking after my son, not him looking after me. I wished Thomas didn't show such impatience when I'd ask him to do basic things before he left for work. I wished he'd take a couple of weeks holiday or long service leave to help out.

I sat in my armchair and wondered what would become of me. I felt like an utter failure. I'd say to Mum and Dad when they came up, 'Please don't work too hard.'

Mum would say, 'It's the least we can do... wish you were closer.'

Mum found the trips exhausting. She had a highly responsible job and no downtime. Dad's medical retirement hadn't lasted long. He began full-time work, but in a much lighter capacity, as a general hand at my brother's work.

I'd say, 'This is too much for you and Dad. I'll organise extra help.'

Mum would say, 'That won't stop your father. He's tired, too, but he insists on coming.'

They were a supreme team; angels in duo. They were the epitome of Good Samaritans. No obstacle was too great for them, and they never gave up until they'd crossed the finishing line. I couldn't keep up with them. All I could do was lovelovelove them and thankthankthank them for their never-ending love and support.

Their response, 'Seeing you get better are all the thanks we need.' Before they'd leave, they hug and kiss and say, 'You'll be back to your old self in no time.'

Although my emotions were chaotic, I had a calm certainty and confidence that I'd get well. On the surface, there were days when the wind whipped up wild skies and the elements tossed my emotions about like worthless flotsam.

Kind friends lent me books. 'You'll have more time to read.'

But reading was impossible. Reading a caption felt equal to reading a novel. I flipped over magazine pages wondering if magazines were really necessary. The television sounded like utter madness and seemed equally non-essential.

In an instinctive way, I began to set up a direct instructional programme for myself. I'd designed programmes for students with special needs, so I set about drawing up my own. I broke down moves into micro moves. For example – how to stand up from a sitting position: step one: sit firmly on chair and place both feet flat on the floor...

I found that the step-by-step instruction helped ground my emotions, too. Each step – each goal reached – was filled with hope and purpose.

Trying to communicate with the left side of my body was like trying to decipher invisible instructions on a blank page and my stroke had a solitary nature. It ignored me. I had to build a rapport with it. After all, we were in this together. I spoke to my left side firmly. 'You can turn your back on me, but I'm not going to turn my back on you.'

Within a few months, I was ready to go to hydrotherapy. Hydrotherapy, once a week, for months helped. Kind friends and neighbours shared the driving to and from the heated pool. As a thank you to my friends, I organised for a small group of us to attend a free six week relaxation course, courtesy of my disability. One instruction which the instructor gave at the beginning of every session was, 'I'd like you to stay awake during the meditation exercises.' But every week, at least one of the group would snore their way to the end.

Eventually, my small walks became longer. Sometimes, it took weeks to make the next advance. Every advance held its own reward: to the back steps, out under the grand old turpentine which sheltered azaleas, camellias, magnolia and ferns; down the back steps; down the sloping path past next door's fish pond and our heavily scented port wine magnolia; down one, then two steps onto the driveway, down to the gutter past three callistemons.

Apparently, surviving this type of bleed was rare. At my appointment with the neurologist, he smiled and said, 'You're going well. It was in your favour that you were young and your veins were in good condition - and way it bled – that's what saved you. Now, keep doing more of the same.'

I was more than thankful because I had a lively seven year old son who needed his mother and, in my down times, he seemed to be my only reason for living.

For the first few months after the CVA, I was very dependent. The first couple of weeks, friends were kind and dropped in meals. As time went on, I'd set veggies out on the bench ready for Thomas when he came home from work.

One afternoon, I thought I'd surprise him. I'd go down to the front to greet him when he drove in after work. He'd be surprised to see me standing there.

When he turned into the driveway, I smiled and waved.

He got out of the car and called out, 'What's wrong?'

'Nothing.' I couldn't stop smiling. 'I managed the side steps. Yay!'

He said, 'I've got a meeting tonight. I won't put the car away.'

Sometimes before his meetings he'd come in and have a shower then leave.

'Will you be here for tea?'

'No.'

'Before you go, would you mind cutting up the veggies and putting them on?'

Thomas walked past me and headed up the side passage. It was reasonably steep with a few steps, which was why it was such a good workout for me; a real achievement.

He hurried up the last few steps and opened the gate. He turned and called back, 'You needn't think I'm doing this every night.'

'I'll need help for a while.'

He stood at the top of the steps and looked down on me. 'Sometimes, I think it would've been better if you'd died.'

I didn't have time to protect myself from the words which were flung so casually.

'What an awful thing to say!'

There was no response, like 'I was only joking,' so I said, 'You know, if I died you'd have to cook every meal.'

I focused on negotiating the next few steps. I'd have time to think about the implications of what my husband had just said later. I knew that my CVA had made our lives raw but I'd heard what I heard. I couldn't unhear it. I was so hurt, but, I wasn't going to let it stop me asking him to do as I'd asked.

When I walked into the kitchen, he was standing there as if waiting for a bus that was running late. He stared directly at the bench where the potatoes, beans and carrots sat on the cutting board. 'So where are they?'

'Right here. I put them here.'

He didn't know it, but his words had put steel rods in my bones. I felt a strength in me like I'd never felt before.

His show of impatience and cruel words were more to do with his fear of change than anything. Also, I was on the move again, no longer sitting helplessly at home, where Thomas had expected me to be.

I'd been so used to listening to Thomas's feelings, I'd learnt to suppress my own. Except for a few special friends, who knew about my difficult situation with Thomas, I'd always balanced life by dining out on moments of beauty and connection with the divine. At certain times of the year, I'd stand in awe, looking out to the ocean through our large front window. The sight of the sun building rungs of Jacob's golden ladder on the ocean's surface, leading up to the heavens, filled me with cheer. I felt I could climb that ladder.

Eventually, I began to refer to my CVA as a Stroke of Good Luck. It gifted me with a clear strong lens. I also relied on a small lens I had, which I'd used to carry with me. It was a kaleidoscope - a deep purple cone about four centimetres by three. I kept it within easy reach, either in my pocket or on the kitchen windowsill.

Whenever I lost hope or needed to calm down or felt depressed, I'd hold it up to my eye and focus on a plant or flower in the back garden. I'd see a repetitive pattern of loveliness. Apart from looking at life from my kaleidoscope's point of view, I employed another trick. I'd put my fingers up to my eyes and peer through them as if I was the Ancient Mariner. I'd look through the slitted fingers which cut out glare. They seemed to filter out noise too. I'd look through the narrow slit and focus on either the ocean or a cloudscape or the treetops.

The amount of effort required to heal from a stroke was enormous. I needed to ensure I took regular rests. My body and mind needed time to handle the profound change which had taken place and the healing which needed to take place. Every day, new steps were taken until I turned into the tortoise I needed to be, and whose carapace could withstand any predator's claws.

## No Looking Back

Before my stroke, our coupledom's social life had always been full. Thomas and I picnicked with friends. We stood around barbecues on carpets of pine needles in groves where filtered light shone through sheltering canopies of pine and eucalypt, under which our children played. There were bushwalks, wildflower walks, sailing on Lake Macquarie with friends. We looked after each other's houses at holiday times: watered gardens, collected mail, fed pets. We were involved in the church. We spent regular weekends in Sydney visiting parents and old friends. We travelled north, south and west on holidays.

We led a full life, but after the stroke my world became smaller. A favourite time of day was to sit out the back of the house by the garden and watch the seasonal impact on the plants. I felt I was part of the change. I shivered when it felt like winter in my garden while those around me frolicked like it was spring.

In the past, I'd learnt to treat personal feelings as a form of selfishness, an indulgence. It was biblical. But after my CVA, something great happened. Insight challenged vows and unpacked all the preachings that lacked love and respect towards mankind.

The paralysis from my leaked malformation had stopped my outer world which enabled the consciousness of my inner world to ripen. It was time to trust that which was within myself. My job was to pause and to listen. I no longer ignored gut feelings. I began to listen to them first.

Once I acknowledged the pain of the loneliness from the lack of companionship over fifteen years, the pain dissolved, just like that. At times, the new me took fright. This was a daring place to be. But courage took me by the hand, and I changed steps. Thomas had to change his, too. I never meant to change the dance so dramatically but my spirit was My Fair Lady and could've danced all night.

I'd sit out the back feeding sparrows. I'd make cups of tea or coffee for well-meaning friends. One acquaintance, a minister's wife, visited me. I didn't know her very well. She was a tall formidable woman with strong opinions. She suggested that one of the reasons I had the stroke could be 'So busy people like me can come and sit here in your lovely garden.'

It was a light-hearted comment but with some truth about timeout. I could see that when she spoke loudly to me it was as if she thought the stroke had left me deaf. I could tell by the manner in which she lent in and exaggerated the enunciation of every syllable she also seemed to believe I had trouble comprehending.

'I. Need. Time. Out,' she said.

She didn't need me to be the other side of the conversation, either. She conversed with herself. Even so, I appreciated the fact that in her busy day she'd taken valuable time out to visit and I understood her need to chill. Been there, done that, but after her visit I began to notice that I was often seen more as an unabled person, not disabled.

Insights like that poured in, and some of them were painful. I began to see and hear things in a hologrammatic way. Life was now cinerama and 360 degrees. Family and friends often talked over and around me and made decisions on my behalf. While my difficulty in walking was obvious, no one could see the exponential growth exploding inside me. I was grateful that my sensitive young son, Paul, would arrive home from school and race into the bedroom and bring the world to me, speaking to the Me in me.

'Mum, Mum, guess what...'

He was lifesaving sunshine.

About ten months after the CVA, the neurologist, Dr T, said it should be fine for me to go back to small singing group in which Thomas and I both sang.

I took up my usual place in the front row with first sopranos. It was a wonderful feeling to be amongst the vibrational harmonies again; and to sing with a unified heart-beat with like-minded souls. It was the best of the very best medicine.

At practice, we stood and sang a couple of songs. I felt a little lightheaded, so sat down. I told myself this was to be expected. It had been a long time; nothing to worry about. That's when I saw Dr T hurry across.

He bent down and said, all apologetic, 'I thought you were an alto.'

'I'm a first soprano but I can sing seconds if-'

'Sorry - sorry, Anne, it's too high – the pitch – the vibrations... no, no. Sorry.'

He was so apologetic it was as if it was his fault that I'd been born a first soprano. I sat out the rest of the practice.

I'd sung most of my life in small amateur capacities. In a magical group at school we sang at ABC concerts and at the Cell Block theatre and chamber music afternoons. After I married, I sang with Thomas in the church choir. I wondered if Dr T was being a touch over protective.

I asked my GP, 'What do you think?'

'I suppose you can go around to different doctors until you find someone who will say what you want to hear. In my opinion, you'd be putting yourself at risk. I don't recommend it but the final decision is yours.'

Thenceforth, Thomas went to all choir practices alone.

Grief, the loss of independence and of the necessary abilities I needed to carry out my roles as wife, mother and Jill-of-all-trades accumulated, so I determined to get them back. Between my two hour sleeps in the morning and afternoons, I exercised but, I tired easily. Even a snail could've beaten me.

There were good and bad hair days. Some days it was a major achievement to simply climb out of bed and climb over the heavy lump of despair which sometimes rolled in when I wasn't looking. I could see for myself that exercise was an invaluable free ticket but it required enormous amounts of persistent self motivation and a positive sense of humour.

    Exercise. Stand up. Sit down. Phew. Exhausted. Rest.

    Lie on bed - straighten good leg. Is the knee straight?

    Copy same action with left leg. No cheating. I said no cheating.

    Leg straight. Straighter. Hold. Good girl. Proud of you. Can't feel a thing - don't worry - one day - one day - even if it's only in the imagination.

    It was up to me to create new neural pathways. No one could do that for me. No one could see that I was also busy stepping over and around inner emotional obstacles. My mind was so quiet. It'd been a long time since I'd heard the chatter of my emotions. I'd developed, somehow, startling clarity which, at first, stunned me. I kept exercising and walking, until I slowly became the determined tortoise I needed to be; emotions in hand.

Spring 1981. My parents had come up again for the weekend to help. I sat in the sunroom and felt guilty as I watched my tired mother set up the ironing board. 'Mum, you don't have to do that. It can wait.'

    'I'll take my time. Every little bit helps.'

    She filled the iron with water and turned on the power. It hissed,

    'Let's go.'

    Paul was in the backyard playing with a couple of friends. They had climbed the big pepper tree up the back and were busily adding an additional platform to the treehouse.

    Dad finished the washing up. He dried his hands on the small kitchen towel and turned to me and said. 'Right, Twerpo, how about you and I go for a drive?'

    'Where to?'

    'Wherever you want.'

'What do you mean?'

'You're taking me for a drive.'

'I can't do that.'

It'd been at least nine months since I'd driven. I was walking more confidently now and had initiated a few things, like getting a cleaner. I arranged to sell my beautiful block of land in the mountains. I'd use the money to fund renovations to the house – new kitchen, laundry, family/garden/sunroom – and convert the old kitchen into a lovely new dining room with large sliding glass doors looking out onto the garden.

It was time for me to stand on my own two feet, but the most restricting thing in my life was not being able to drive. Friends had encouraged me to try but Thomas assured me I'd not be driving again, and the fearful part of me believed him.

'Dad, I can't drive.'

'Yes, you can.'

'I can't.'

I looked at Mum, who shrugged. 'You know your father.'

Mum was probably as scared as me and every time I looked at her I saw how tired she was. These weekends away were exhausting both of them.

I'd repeat, 'Mum, don't come if you're too tired.'

'If it was up to me –'

Mum had a highly responsible job managing a staff of twenty-four in her department. She loved her work. Dad had retired as a bus driver/starter because of illness and was doing light duties, as a general hand, at my brother's work. His advanced emphysema prevented him from doing much more.

Driving was Dad's salvation. If anyone understood the fear of losing one's independence it was him. Some days, he was so puffed he could hardly get in and out of the car and here he was offering me my independence.

Thomas was out for the afternoon, but Dad said we could use his car, which was the same model Renault as ours. 'C'mon. Let's get a move on.'

'Dad, are you game?'

'I'm game if you're game.'

'Not really. What if something happens?'

'Well - it'll happen to both of us.'

'What if I - ?'

'Nothing's going to happen.'

Dad had taught me to drive when I was younger and he knew what a nervous Nellie I've been back then but I turned out to be a natural driver just like him. It was just that as an L plater I was demanding a 100% guarantee that nothing would happen. I was asking for much the same now.

'But you don't know -'

'Look - a man hasn't got all day. It's like riding a bike – you never forget.'

'I'm not good at riding bikes.'

'Well, it's like riding a horse – giddy-up.'

'Dad - this is serious.'

'C'mon, you'll be right.'

And with that one loving intervention, I got my driving wheels back, and more confidence.

When we came home and after I'd successfully parked the car, I sat back and sighed. 'Dad, I can't thank you enough. This is epic - this is - I never thought -'

'Okay. You're on your way now, so no looking back. I'll be onto you if you do.'

I leant over and kissed him on the cheek. 'Got it.'

We walked inside and Mum looked flushed. There was the heat from the steam iron but she'd obviously been concerned.

'How did she go?'

'Just as we expected. Like a trooper.'

I loved the way they smiled at each other. It said, 'I love you and mission accomplished.' Dad bent over the ironing board and kissed Mum sweetly on the lips. They'd moved mountains, again.

Dad said, 'Who'd like a cuppa? A man needs a drink after that.'

When Thomas arrived home, I told him the good news.

'Guess what? Dad took me for a drive. Can you believe it? I can drive.'

Thomas looked to Dad, to Mum, to me.

Ever the pedant, Dad said, 'You mean, you took your old man for a drive. I didn't take you.' He turned to Thomas and said, 'Mate, she drove like a trooper.' Dad's eyes shone.

Thomas's elbows gripped his sides. 'Good,' he said and walked inside.

By now, Dad had instilled so much confidence in me that in spite of Thomas's deafening silent scream of disapproval, I knew I'd been given back my driving life, which would ease my parents workload.

After they left, Thomas said, 'I don't like the thought of you driving.'

'I'm allowed to.'

'But you still have a limp.'

'Have I? I didn't know I had one. Oh, well, never mind. I'll be the driver with a limp.'

Taken-for-granted things held the greatest thrill in the next step of my recovery. I never thought I'd get excited about wiping down kitchen benches or cleaning the kitchen sink but I did. It was one achievement after another. Both sides of the body now worked in sync, though the right side would always have to bear more of the heavy lifting than the left side, but, hey, I was driving again.

# Painting White Roses

1983. On our next weekend visit to Sydney, to see our parents, Thomas headed into town for a few hours while I drove myself to a favourite china painting outlet close by. As the car wheels turned, I gave thanks for the ability to drive. I gave thanks that I had my independence back. I gave thanks that I could walk without thinking.

As I walked into the china painting shop, my heart filled with the staff's warm welcome. The simple most minuscule things like choosing china pieces to paint, or buying the latest enthusiast magazine, felt exhilarating. But, would I still have my painter's eye? What would my fine motor skills be like? Would my finger / thumb intelligence still be there?

I needn't have worried. Surprisingly, my focus and painter's eye came back sharper than before. While, for months, the brushes didn't move as well, my eye for detail was more intense, possibly because I'd been living in a small world, like the world of the snail and tortoise.

In slow time, I'd inhabited the small world. When in recovery, sitting out the back or sitting on the front veranda, slow-time revealed the marvel of magnificence around me, such as, the beauty in the spread of a sparrow's wings just as it takes flight.

I wanted to paint white roses. It was something I'd intended to do pre-stroke. It was the ultimate china painting challenge. I'd have to capture subtleties of tone, temperature and texture and light and shade - white on white. As I laid out the composition of the foundational roses and leaves on the plate, I rediscovered old pathways in my brain and made new ones.

I noticed that my energy tanks emptied quickly. The simplest painting strokes required high levels of concentration. I had to be patient and trust that I'd get my mental and physical strength back. The secret was to stop before I got tired. Tiredness quickly turned into overtiredness. I learnt to paint for twenty minutes then refuel – rest – refuel – rest. If I went too long, it'd take days to refuel.

The large white plate was heavy to hold but painting white on white, white roses on a soft white glaze, filled me with joy. I felt more alive than ever.

One day, I was painting when I began to feel nauseous – not only in the morning but all day. I suspected I might be pregnant. I remembered we'd just celebrated Thomas's forty second birthday a few weeks earlier. Our parents had come up and we'd had the best night.

I'd prepared a three course meal and we sat around the dining table talking and laughing for hours. It was one of those nights where there was a special light in the room and the room was full of love. When it came time for us to go to bed, Thomas created a funny scene about a husband and his due on his birthday. He took my arm and we walked out of the living room while everyone laughed. When we reached the bedroom, Thomas called back to our guests, 'Good night,' and closed the door with some ceremony. The night had the magic of earlier more innocent days.

Anyway, surprisingly, I was pregnant. It didn't seem possible. I was delighted and conflicted. I sat in the chair opposite Dr F, who immediately rang the neurologist, Dr T. Questions about my previous CVA went back and forth. How could I tell them not to worry? How could I explain to them my pumpkin dream?

*I watch a flourishing pumpkin grow in the backyard. It's morning. I look into water drops on the voluminous green leaves which seem to be waltzing. Bees are busy among brilliant yellow trumpets. I see a pumpkin; light-filled, fulsome, polished. I wake with its glowing image and know I'm going to have a baby girl.*

At the time, the more rational, sceptical side of me doubted that very much. Yet, even after my stroke recovery, with all logic and rational intention in hand, the memory of the dream persisted. In ensuing years, I'd convinced myself it was a dream I had to let go.

Dr T spoke to me on the phone's loudspeaker. 'It means you'd have to support an extra bloodstream... putting your own blood system under pressure... no guarantee... dangerous. We don't know what's happened to the malformation. My suspicion is it's sealed itself off - might have rerouted - we can only hope so but I can't say. Anne, I'd encourage you to think seriously. You were lucky the first time - there's no saying - have you considered not going ahead?'

'I want to go ahead.'

Dr F asked, 'Could you recommend someone?'

As they spoke, I had within me a fulsome, glowing image and a strong light-filled knowing that I'd have a healthy baby girl.

Dr T said, 'She'll need someone who can keep an eye on a few things... R is semi-retired - only takes complicated cases these days. Let's see if we can get him.'

The semi-retired obstetrician, Dr R, was a marvellous choice. He was clever, kind and droll; a koala of a man with a strong soft soul; just what I needed.

He said, 'It's not a surprise really. A life-threatening event can affect the partner, too. It's the body's way of recognising an urgent need to reproduce.'

He said the most important thing for me now was to lead a quiet, uneventful life. I looked forward to that but, to my amazement, and after all these years, Thomas came home one afternoon and announced that he'd been offered a promotion in Sydney. 'It's the position I've always wanted.'

We'd been in Newcastle fourteen years. While it was the worst time for me to consider a move, considering my closely monitored pregnancy and supposed quiet life, it would be wonderful to be back near family and old friends. It could be an answer to prayer, so all I needed to do was take extra care.

The next few weeks were exhausting: preparing the house for sale, packing. We decided to leave most of our furniture in the house until we purchased in Sydney and our current house was settled. We stayed with my parents, setting up in my old bedroom in Artarmon Road. We slept on a borrowed double bed mattress on the floor.

I settled Paul into his new school at Artarmon and faced real estate agents and attended consultations with the clinically mannered obstetrician opposite the Royal North Shore Hospital, the hospital I once knew so well.

We found a potential home in North Epping, close to schools and transport with a lovely big bushy reserve out the back. I could see big family fun days there. After we paid the holding deposit, someone was very quiet.

I asked Thomas, 'Is something wrong?'

In recent weeks, he'd headed off to work with a frown which grew deeper and deeper until it was a furrow. The move, like any move, was going to be difficult but, like Thomas, I, too, faced challenges so assumed he'd gradually settle. Thomas hated the change so much he asked to be transferred back.

'In Newcastle, I'm not answerable to anyone. Most of these guys are uni graduates... dog eat dog - nothing like Newcastle.'

The sale of our house was cancelled and within weeks we transferred back. I'd be forever grateful to all my friends who rallied and helped unpack boxes.

While I would love to have stayed in Sydney, nothing was going to change Thomas's mind. I immediately went back to Dr R, my obstetrician. He was the plus side to the move back. I felt far more comfortable with him.

He walked out to greet me and we walked together along the long hallway. He said, 'Can you do that again - walk back down the hall and come back again - I want to see something.'

He stood at the end of the hallway and watched. He smiled then ushered me into his surgery. He asked what I'd been doing. I told him about the move, some of which he would've already known because he'd been in touch with my Sydney obstetrician.

He gave me a check-up and said, 'You look like the Leaning Tower of Pisa. I know it hasn't toppled yet but you're about to and we can't take that risk. You need rest.'

I was admitted to hospital that day. The rest of the week passed quickly.

Dr R said, 'I'd like you to stay a little longer.'

'My son's going to be on school holidays.'

But Dr R insisted. Fortunately, Paul was much loved and he enjoyed endless sleepovers, outings and mini holidays here and there.

At Christmas, I was allowed home for two days. In the New Year, I felt strong, so I asked if I could go home.

Dr R said, 'Let's take it a day at a time. Let's start with one day. Next Saturday.'

Saturday came. I was so excited. I had my breakfast and went to lie back down and roll to one side. That's when there was a landslide. My head spun and spun. I couldn't see. I pressed the buzzer.

Dr T was away. His replacement was notified and eventually arrived. He'd obviously been dragged out of bed. He looked and smelt like he'd had a heavy night. He inspected my ears so roughly that he caused one of them to bleed. He seemed oblivious to how difficult it was for a ripe pumpkin to roll over and lie on its back, with its head hanging off the end of the bed, when nine months pregnant.

He twisted my head from side to side. Vertigo went wild. Still couldn't see. Stemotil injection; sides of the bed put up; spinning, spinning, praying for calm. Dear Lord, please, please don't let anything happen - we're so close.

Options were discussed. The baby was a good size so the Caesarean was moved forward a week. I rested and everything settled. When I could, I'd walk the long hospital corridors, trying to stay a few steps ahead of fear, even though, these days, there was an inner calm and I'd learnt to trust it.

From my room, I could see Newcastle Ocean Baths and the glorious stretch of the Pacific beyond. Every morning, I read 'Eternity' written in the smooth sand in copperplate, similar to Arthur Stacy's 'Eternity' which he'd dedicated himself to write on the footpaths of Sydney for thirty-five years.

I'd stand on the small balcony and watch waves crash. My baby and I were part of the incoming tide. I was overwhelmed with gratitude for being in such an oasis of care and beautiful landscape.

'Thank you, Lord, thank you.'

I ordered extra food and blamed the smell of salt water for my porky appetite. I could've eaten the menu. I stored extra food in plastic containers in the drawers so as to not share it with the hungry mini beasts who were shy permanent residents who scampered about in the occasional hospital drawer and cupboard.

My parents were due to arrive from Sydney anytime now. Mum had recently retired at sixty-nine. She could've kept working but Dad was already retired and needed full-time care and attention. He was too puffed out these days to put on his own shoes. That's where Mum wanted to be and, on a brighter note, they had a new grandchild on the way and wanted to be there for the birth.

Early in the morning on Thursday 2 February 1984, my young hairdresser arrived to cut my hair before she went to work. After she left, I headed to the bathroom. I intended to have a shower and wash my hair but my back muscles spasmed. I couldn't move. I rang the bell and two nurses came.

'It feels as though my spine's unzipped - I can't stand.'

'Are you in labour?'

'I wouldn't call it pain - it's more like twinges.'

'Are you timing them?'

'No. I'm not due for a couple of weeks.'

'Baby's a good size - it's anytime now.'

The nurses helped me back into bed and put on a monitor and, yes. I was in the first stages of labour. Dr R came and booked a caesar in for later that day.

By late afternoon, my parents had arrived and brought Paul with them. Thomas arrived after work. I was due to go to theatre at nine thirty p.m. The family followed me when I was wheeled to the lift. My thoughts were - am I going to survive this? As the lift doors closed, I thought - will I ever see them again? I wished I could've taken the worry out of my parents' eyes. They shared similar thoughts.

When I was wheeled into theatre, it sounded like someone was having a party. I wished my family could've been there. Neurologists, heart specialists, anaesthesiologists along with one or two curious who asked for permission to be there, smiled as I was put on the operating table.

The atmosphere was celebratory, like the moment before the cake's cut. Before I drifted off, I counted thirteen souls around the bed. We were all in this together with every precaution being taken. God willing, soon there'd be another soul to join in the celebration.

Rebecca Anne Mary was born a strong healthy baby at nine fifty-five pm in the Royal Newcastle Hospital. Weight eight pounds. Height fifty-six centimetres. In Recovery, they held her close for me to see. I pulled a resistant eyelid open. Our daughter was swaddled in white. Only her face and hands were visible. A holy sight. I reached out and touched the most elegant fingers and they curled around mine.

'You're so beautiful.'

She was still powder-white from the womb and perfect. She looked like my childhood doll, Baby Doll, with the same profile, eyelashes, cheeks and Cupid mouth. And it wasn't a dream. We were both alive.

'Thank you, Lord, thank you.'

Next morning, I was wheeled back to my room where a proud father, brother, grandparents and baby were waiting.

Dad said, 'I've never said so many Hail Mary's in all my life. I'm surprised I could remember them.'

'Just as well,' I said.

On change of shifts, Night and Day Sisters argued. Day Sister insisted that baby didn't need supplements day or night. But Night Sister felt that a supplement was sometimes necessary so the mother could have a decent sleep. Day Sister said the mother's milk was coming in nicely so should not be interfered with and that mother and baby had settled well. Night Sister said the obstetrician left instructions that the mother needed deep sleeps. Day Sister said the mother had at least two sound sleeps during the day and that should be sufficient.

One night, I woke and reached out to touch Rebecca's crib. I couldn't find it. Where was it? I slipped out of bed, eyes half open and headed for the nursery, managing to crash into the door on the way.

Night Sister heard the commotion and came running. 'She's fine. Back to bed. Still a couple of hours.'

On day three, I sat by the window aware that I was also out there, part of a seismic shift, of being held umbilically; a birthing star. Tears welled. Senses were on high alert. The earth breathed. Breasts swelled. Milk tides. I submitted myself to the wondrous pool of life and wept and wept.

Word spread around the hospital about the miracle baby and mother. Interested doctors, family and friends visited.

When it came time to leave, there were fond farewells. Day Sister looked pleased. She was probably relieved she could once more regain control of her floor.

In times past, I'd walked out of hospital with empty arms, but this time I floated alongside proud father and son. They were loaded up with weeks of luggage and presents. I was grounded by arm hugging gratitude for the small miracle I held in my arms.

Before we climbed into the car, I took a long look across the road at the zinging blue of the ocean merging with the blue of the sky. There was no horizon to speak of, just the sound of destined waves arriving from distant shores. Undercurrents moved unseen, obeying the ever present pull of the moon.

# A Daughter of Eve

I'd been told that 'women's issues,' as they were referred to, would disappear after my daughter's birth. Not so. Becca was two years old when I was in need of an urgent hysterectomy. It'd been five years since my CVA and two years since I'd given birth by Caesearan section under a full anaesthetic. I assumed I'd have one for the hysterectomy but the anaesthetist said, 'It's your stroke history that concerns me. You'll have to have an epidural. I can't risk you having a full anaesthetic. I'll give you a sedative. If you feel stressed during the operation, I can give you more.'

I didn't want any complications but the thought of being wide awake didn't appeal.

As I waited outside the operating theatre to go in my surgeon, Dr R, came out. 'I'm sorry. I didn't expect that.'

But, whenever I opened my eyes during the procedure, the anaesthetist was there. He'd smile and almost immediately I'd drift back to sleep.

In Recovery, I shivered. I was like a bag of bones rattling. No amount of warm blankets helped so the nurses turned a heater, like a two-bar radiator, on its back under the bed to warm me up. I cried, too, which surprised me.

One nurse said, 'Why are you crying?'

'I don't know.'

Maybe it was shock. At that moment, I wished I'd been given a full anaesthetic but there was a real benefit from having the epidural.

Compared to my room-mates, who'd had full anaesthetics on the same day, I recovered more quickly.

I was in a ward with three other women, in a pleasant new private hospital at Warner's Bay. We looked out through large windows onto a lovely garden area. My parents had travelled up from Sydney to help look after the children. Thomas visited me on the first night after my operation and I introduced him to my friendly room-mates.

I didn't see him again until the day before I came home. He walked into the ward looking fresh and business-like in his whiter than white shirt, striped tie, light grey trousers and black leather shoes. Before he greeted me, he walked around the ward and greeted each room-mate. He enquired after their health. I was proud of him when I saw that each one of them was left beaming after his attention.

He came over to me and leant close. He pressed his lips onto mine then whispered, 'It's my lunch hour. I don't have time for this.'

In that very second, a voice within me said, 'One day, you'll leave this man.' I was shocked by its certainty.

Thomas whispered, 'I can't stay. I don't have time.'

Before he left, he waved to the room. Everyone smiled and waved back.

He called out, 'Love you, sweetheart.'

I played the game, waved and smiled.

After he'd gone, the patient in the bed next to me said, 'You're a lucky woman having a man like that.'

Thomas had organised three days off to help me after the hysterectomy. I was relieved because my parents had come up to help. It meant he could lighten their load. I didn't want them getting overtired.

As I was packing my bag to go home, expecting Thomas to arrive any minute, Mum walked in.

'Hello. I thought Thomas was picking me up.'

'He said he's got a bit of a bug - gastric or something.'

We walked out to the car which was outside the front door of the hospital. Dad had the car idling. After we hopped in, Mum said, 'I don't know what we're going to do with you.'

'What do you mean?'

'Well, your father and I put fresh linen on your bed this morning, and we suggested to Thomas that because he's got a bug of some sort, it'd might be best if he slept out on the divan. That way, you won't catch what he's got.'

Dad said, 'The last we saw of the silly coot, he was lying on the bed.'

'I'm sorry but you might have to sleep out on the divan. How do you feel about that? I can't think of what else to do.'

Thomas's action was an eye-opener for my parents but it wasn't for me. 'Don't worry. I'll sleep on the divan.'

It was another one of his games. It seemed hard to believe that Thomas had disrespected my parents, and so deliberately, because he seemed to be genuinely fond of them, and was always on his best behaviour around them.

Dad was unusually tight-lipped on the way home and Mum sounded exhausted. She sighed and coughed, as if trying to clear her throat, tight with disappointment in the young man in whom she'd placed so much trust and hope.

In the past, whenever I'd make the slightest squeak about how hard it was living with Thomas, she used to say, 'Marriage's hard work. You have to give more than take.'

I knew that. I'd followed that credo but there was only so much one person could do.

When we arrived home, Thomas sent a message to me via my parents. 'I don't want you to get my infection, sweetheart.'

I slept in the dining room on the low-slung rubber divan.

In spite of the inconvenience of getting in and out of such a low bed, with a wound, my recovery was excellent. I'd been blessed with good healing genes and the loving care of my parents. Soon, it was time for them to go home. It was always difficult to express to them just how grateful I was .

After the operation, I thrived. It was a wonderful new feeling and, in time, I felt better than I had in years.

Thomas continued to go to committee meetings and other activities. Some nights, he'd come home later than usual and be quite frisky. Either I'd be in bed reading or have the lights out and was half asleep.

One night, after I turned away from his friskiness, he jumped out of bed and turned on the main light. He stormed out of the room and reappeared holding one of the window rods from the sunroom. He stood at the end of the bed and proceeded to thrash it around. He hit the bed close to my toes, but mostly he swirled it around his head and in front of his chest. I dared not move.

'What are you doing?'

'You're my wife.'

'I know.'

'And if I want-'

The rod swished up and down, side to side. I was scared, but my gut feeling was it was an act. Thomas didn't hit me physically, but emotionally, he was hitting his target.

How to de-escalate? How to distract?

The children were asleep.

I whispered, 'Thomas, why don't you go and have a shower and then -'

He held the rod in mid-air not too sure of his next move. He walked out into the hallway and I heard the rod drop onto the floor. The bathroom door slammed shut. Soon, I heard the shower running.

I climbed out of bed, picked up the rod and put it back on the windowsill where it belonged. I turned out the main light and slipped back into bed. I reached across and turned on Thomas's bedside lamp, turned off mine and curled up into a ball. My mind raced. Did fake rage ever cross the line into out-of-control rage?

Soon, Thomas slipped into bed and fell sound asleep. I spent the night mentally packing up the family and I couldn't imagine what would happen when, one day, I'd have to say that we needed to separate, for everyone's sake. It'd raise the stakes exponentially. My gut had already told me that I was the one who'd have to make the first move.

One night in bed, about a week later, Thomas made a declaration into the dark.

'If I get AIDS, it's your fault... because of your transfusion.'

He didn't know it but, after the rod incident the other night, his declaration was tapping into a growing fear of mine.

I sat up, turned on the light and said, 'I've never had a transfusion so you can stop worrying.'

At times, Thomas's night fears would wake us. On this night, it was his fear of catching AIDS.

He insisted, 'You did have a transfusion.'

'I didn't.'

'When you had the miscarriage.'

'That was ten years ago. I signed papers for a transfusion but I didn't have one. I can assure you, that if you get AIDS, it won't be because of me.'

'What do you mean?'

'I mean, why are you suddenly worrying about AIDS. It's got nothing to do with me.'

'If I get it, it will be because of you.'

I could've reminded him about a singular time, before we had children, when he gave me something which also had nothing to do with me. It was one of those humiliating experiences.

We were trying to fall pregnant and, at the time, I was keeping a temperature chart which showed the more fertile times of the month. At one stage, I thought I had a form of cystitis, so I immediately went to the GP.

Dr. F was so gentlemanly. He didn't actually spell out what I had. Possibly, he assumed I knew but I didn't. He skirted around the subject and said things like, 'Are you having a relationship with someone else other than your husband?'

'No.'

'You'll need to check Thomas's... and if... I'll give you some scripts.'

I took the scripts to our local chemist, who was a close friend of Thomas. When he dispensed the meds, he looked over the dispensary wall and frowned at me. Usually, an assistant dealt with sales but instead he came round and served me then he walked out of the shop with me. We stood a few metres away from the shop entrance.

He spoke quietly in a deep chastising tone. 'I'm very disappointed in you.'

I looked at him and he pointed to the bag of goods I held.

'It's not fair on Thomas.'

What was he talking about? What wasn't fair? I frowned at his look of disgust, and then it clicked. This must be one of those unmentionable things.

I was insulted. This tall man standing, as if over me, assumed I was the guilty party. I shot back, 'This has nothing to do with me.'

He rolled his eyes at this daughter of Eve, standing there, supposedly in brash denial. With a huff of disgust, he turned around and walked away, back into the pharmacy.

When I checked Thomas that night, he thought it was hilarious. I found what the doctor had described and he laughed even more.

'You obviously got it off a toilet seat and you've given it to me. Oh, sweetheart, you're so naive.'

I have to be kind to my naive self, because, even then, I was prepared to be convinced that I might have caught it off a toilet seat, after all. That was a common tale at the time. Fortunately, years later, when lying in bed with Thomas telling me that I might give him AIDS, I wasn't as naive. I was realistic enough to know that if he caught AIDS it would, most definitely, have nothing to do with me. It was time. This man, my husband, was possibly risking my life, as well as his.

Dirty laundry, indeed.

'Thomas, you won't get AIDS from me. Okay?'

'You don't know that.'

'I do know that.'

Rather than falling asleep on that particular night, I waited till Thomas fell asleep then I slipped out of bed. I made a late supper of toast and Vegemite and a cup of hot Milo to help settle my crazy early morning thoughts, and to soothe my churning stomach which seemed to have a raging pulse of its own.

Fears surfaced as early wild morning thoughts. In the small hours, I remembered that earlier in the night we'd been listening to an AIDS report on the news. Thomas got up from his recliner and walked in and out, while I listened. I suspected it was that which had triggered him.

The news reported that there was a second wave of AIDS. The rising death toll was coming from unexpected quarters: intimate partner transmission between husband and wife.

Thomas was easily triggered under normal circumstances. I'd begun wondering if his rod thrashing the other night had signified a realistic fear of AIDS for him. I hated thinking like that, but my gut screamed, do something. ASAP.

To me, it had become more obvious that Thomas needed to be free to be with his own tribe. Whenever I raised the subject, he was in denial. I knew he'd never leave the marriage, willingly. It was up to me to be the one who'd have to find a safer, happier place, for all of us. My real concerns were with his past history. I feared his frightening actions would escalate.

Later that week, after the children had gone to bed, I said, 'Thomas, let's get some help. The other night with the rod – that was scary.'

He laughed. 'I was letting off steam.'

'It can't happen again.'
'That's up to you.'
'What do you mean?'
'Well - you know.'
'Will you come with me if I organise counselling?'
No answer.
'Will you come?'

Earlier in the week, I've been to see my GP and had told him about the rod incident and about my urgent need to speak with someone.

He'd advised me, years earlier, to consider leaving the marriage. He'd said, 'I think you're in a bad situation there.'

At times, I'd escape into an 'if only' dream where Thomas and I would sit down and bring about a peaceful resolution. I knew our lines.

Thomas: Sweetheart, I can't go on like this. He'd collapse into his recliner and I'd offer to help him wipe up his suffering. He'd say, I can't do this anymore.

I'd say, 'I know.' I'd reach across and pat his arm. 'We can sort something out. Let's focus on what's good between us... we can work around... and the children... and... '

Around that time, there was a life-saving, inspiring new program on ABC Radio National, Caroline Jones – *Search for Meaning*. I didn't know it was going to be the door through which I'd step and learn how to face my fears and take courage. I listened to it in the bedroom, away from the TV. I didn't want to miss a word.

Thomas would walk in and out, in and out. 'What are you listening to?'

'Interviews about people's lives. It's very interesting.'

If he'd known how empowering these stories were, how they gave me guidance, courage, and strength, he wouldn't have approved. Fortunately, Caroline Jones's mellifluous voice sounded innocent enough.

During the interviews, I heard ordinary people tell extraordinary stories of resilience and bravery under exceptional circumstances. There was a marvellous shared spirit and diverse beliefs, and it all came back to one thread - love - an invisible net of love that was out there to support us. I'd already felt upheld by its safety net. I could identify with these guests. I was stunned how they shared so openly. I'd been taught not to talk about private things. But part of overcoming fear was being brave.

I listened to stories where it appeared to be a devastating life situation but when they leant on love and courage it enriched their lives. Guests spoke about their personal growth and how they found beauty and love everywhere, in spite of fearful obstacles. They spoke about the deep sense of compassion they developed for others. So, it could be done. I could leave my marriage but I'd have to be brave.

Many of their stories had similarities to mine; some were far, far worse. For years, I'd knowingly, and sometimes unknowingly, abandoned myself. I thought my only option was to stay and try harder.

Another part of my problem was pride. I didn't like failure. I believed that any problem could be resolved if I just put in a little more love and effort. But, I had to learn that, in the wrong hands, your strength can become your weakness.

# Sick Leave

A definitive moment came one sunny afternoon, after I'd picked up Paul from school. I'd strapped Becca into the car and driven into town, via the scenic road. After we picked up Paul, Thomas suggested we go to the lookout in King Edward Park.

He often drove there to look at the Bogey Hole. It was a lovely view out to the ocean, in a beautiful setting, but always he liked to stand at a very sad place, at the safety fence, which had small bouquets of flowers tied to it, some with sympathy cards, attached. Some flowers and cards were old and some were new. Thomas had mentioned years ago that it was a well-known meeting place for closet gays, and a place where there'd been many gay suicides.

On this day, he said, 'I'd like to see the surf.'

I could understand that. We'd driven in on the scenic route and saw the beauty of the breaking waves. I intended to drive slowly through the park then come out the other side but Thomas asked me to stop at the top.

Usually, I was the one who wanted to stop and smell the roses but this time it was Thomas. He hopped out of the car and was the first one to reach the safety fence. Some people stood by the fence and chatted. These days, I always felt reassured when other people were around, but soon everyone moved on which left us standing there in a strong onshore wind.

With one swift move, Thomas legged the safety fence. My fear flew over to him. Below him, the waves crashed. I looked around hoping for an angel or two.

I called out, 'Thomas, what are you doing? Thomas, the children. Thomas, please.'

He smiled. 'It's okay.'

'You could slip.'

Thomas turned round and held out both his arms, in a welcoming gesture, to Becca. 'C'mon, sweetheart.'

Becca was standing close to me, so at the speed of light I took her hand and headed towards the car. If Thomas did slip, I couldn't bear for her to see it.

I called, 'Paul, C'mon. Hop in the car, please.'

Paul watched his father carefully. 'Dad, come on.'

Thomas took a closer step to the edge.

Paul called, 'Dad, come on.'

I needed to break the loop. I called out loudly, 'Surf's not great today.'

A total lie, but the distraction worked. Paul turned and headed towards the car.

'Seat belts on, please.'

It was always an orchestration with Thomas, but I feared that, one day, something could go terribly wrong. My psychologist had warned me. 'He could take all of you, directly or indirectly.'

Having to turn a terrifying abnormal situation into something seemingly normal, until everyone felt safe, was utterly exhausting and never ceased to set off my terror alarm.

I called out, 'Thomas, we're going.'

I was disturbed and disgusted with his calculated use of terror. He probably had no intention of jumping but he was prepared to risk his daughter's life. What if his foot had slipped on the small loose stones on the very edge and what if -?

It also distressed me that our son had fallen into his father's terror traps too often, another good reason for me to take final steps.

Thomas climbed back over the safety fence. He didn't say a word but when he got into the car he smirked. Maybe it was a smirk of relief that he wasn't lying at the bottom of the cliff in a mangled mess. Step one for me was to drive out of the park. Step two: head for home. Step three: don't think, don't feel.

Now, it was no longer a case of when, but, how soon. I had an additional heavy layer to deal with: the church, the institutional patriarchy; an uncomfortable place for any woman who needed to leave a marriage; to be the protector of her family. I had lovely friends in the church but I didn't know how much I could or should tell them. I'd been a keeper of secrets for years, faithful and loyal. No one would really understand and I didn't want to be part of a blame game or expect people to choose camps.

With fear and foreboding, I made an urgent appointment with Geoff. This telling would be the start of something unimaginable but I couldn't be on the frontline, on my own, any more.

The psychologist's rooms were at the historic end of town, close to the ocean. Before I entered the stately old building, I turned and looked at the wide stretch of beach. I longed to be down there in the shallows paddling and greeting small waves. I wondered if breaking waves knew they fulfilled a purpose when they arrived. Soon, I'd be cresting a wave like that, that is, if I was brave enough to enter this building. I stood by the lift and fragile courage pressed the ancient brass button.

I can't remember whether I took the lift or not. I suspect I walked up the stairs after I heard the lift's metallic moans and groans as it inched its way down to the ground floor. I remember being upstairs and looking out of the windows at restored old dwellings, with backyards almost too small to accommodate the red, yellow and green bins necessary to hold the rubbish of the twentieth century.

My heart thumped. I'd been here, years earlier, for advice but stopped coming because I thought I could try harder to make the marriage work. When I walked into the windowless waiting room with a sixty-watt globe struggling to throw light into the room's dark recesses, I knew I couldn't put off the inevitable any longer.

I sat down in the empty room and busied myself drying my sweaty palms with a small white handkerchief.

Eventually, a tall lean man, with thinning salt and pepper hair, appeared and smiled. It was Geoff, the clinical psychologist.

'Come on in.'

'Thank you.'

As I walked past him, I knew that in the next hour, Geoff would ask me to climb Everest. There was a large old desk and straight-backed chairs in the room. He indicated where I should sit. The eyelids of his greyish eyes drooped a little at the sides, which gave him a look of endless kindness. He spoke as if we were in a library. And, in a sense, we were. There would've been so many stories told in this room and had the stories ever been transcribed, they would've filled a library.

Geoff sat with a notepad on his lap and pen at the ready. I wondered if I should warn him that he might have to write volumes. There was the lookout event, the rod incident and the terror of taking Becca, all evidence of Thomas's acceleration in his attempts to control his environment.

We talked about the suddenness of the lookout incident and how frightening it was and how shocked I was that Thomas even considered thinking about holding his daughter near the edge and outside the safety fence. We discussed the rod incident and my concern with its possible link to Thomas's activities. Then I wept and wept.

Geoff squirmed in his chair before he warned, 'If something like that rod incident ever happens again, I'm afraid you might have to give in for your own safety. Who knows how far he -'

'I don't think I could.'

I teared up, again. He hadn't heard the worst yet - Becca's abduction.

We made another urgent appointment then Geoff said, 'So, you know what you have to do.'

'Separate.' I wept again.

'Do you think Thomas might be willing to come in? How would you feel about that?'

'If he knows I want to leave him, he'll freak out. He has everything to lose.'

'Okay, then, before we do anything, we'll get things sorted just in case you have to leave earlier.'

While part of me was scared, there was an instant physical release. As I drove home, my four-month thumping headache evaporated and the sky seemed bluer. I still lived with fear, and was always on high alert, but I trusted the process.

# The Immolation

Geoff had said in an earlier consultation that when I decided to separate, support would come from my family. He said, 'Ninety-five per cent of families stick together at times like this. You should ask them.'

My family was not in a situation to help. Dad was terminally ill and Mum was exhausted. She looked after him 24/7 and she had serious heart issues of her own. There was no way I could ask them. I didn't live close to any siblings. I had another family, though - my special friends.

These days, I kept the car keys in my pocket, at all times, even when I went to bed, because Thomas's last attempt at suicide had involved Becca, our daughter. It happened just days after his nightmare AIDS talk.

The lookout incident, the rod and Becca's abduction happened so close together that I'd wake up of a morning dreading what the day could bring but I had to keep on an even keel even though I reeled at the escalation of events.

Thomas's last attempt, a couple of days earlier, was on an innocent sunny Saturday afternoon. We were all occupied except Thomas. As it turned out, he was more occupied than I thought. He kept wandering in and out, in and out, as I emptied the kiln. I was finishing a few pieces for an exhibition the following weekend and the sunroom table was littered with half-finished pieces. Paul was surfing with mates. Becca was sitting on the rug near me building a new farm yard out of Lego and settling her newest pony onto the farm. I'd almost emptied the kiln when I noticed Becca was unusually quiet. When I turned to see what she'd done with her pony, she wasn't there.

This was unexpected. After some of her father's actions, she rarely left my side, except to go to preschool or to play next door. I was still unnerved by the lookout and rod incidents. I didn't know what was happening but I knew it involved Becca. Where was she and where was Thomas?

She hadn't wandered out into the backyard because our sunroom had three glass walls and I could see easily if she was out there. I raced through the house. I called her. No answer. In an instant, I knew Thomas had to taken her from the sunroom. I didn't see or hear him take her. I just knew. I called her again. No answer.

The wave of panic I felt was capable of knocking the house down. I heard the car start in the garage downstairs. I raced out onto the front porch and looked down to see Thomas reversing rapidly out of the driveway. He didn't look up. When he drove away, I saw Becca sitting in her car seat.

I raced in and rang the police, neighbours and friends. Everyone went to look for them while I stayed home near the phone in case they came home and/or waited for any news. My world went blank. If you'd asked me what day it was, I couldn't say. There were no mobile phones, so it was a matter of hours before I saw Thomas's close friend drive up the street and park out the front with Thomas and Becca in the car. Becca was safe.

With overwhelming relief, I watched her climb out. I held her and could see the stain of salty dry tears on her cheeks. She was very damp, possibly from being unable to go and pee. I hugged my precious darling and we went inside. I cleaned her and changed her clothes, all the while feeling anger and disgust at Thomas, who was walking slowly up the driveway with his mate.

I couldn't bear to look at him. How dare he! How dare he use our innocent darling daughter as a pawn! How dare he use her as a weapon! For Becca's sake, I had to keep calm.

Thomas's friend had guessed where he might be - somewhere near a railway line. Only another rail enthusiast would think of that, and, thankfully, he was right. When we met up in the kitchen, he said, 'I saw the car inching its way along the road by the water's edge.'

It appears that Thomas had been driving near the ferry wharf, parallel to the train tracks at the end of town, with only a footpath and a few rocks between the car and the industrial mouth of the Hunter River.

A shattered and grateful me went to thank our friend when Thomas walked past with a sheepish grin. He said, 'I'm going to lie down.'

His friend said, 'I'll be off then. Take care, eh?'

Thomas walked inside and I said to our hero, 'Thank you so much. I'm so grateful.'

He looked me in the eye and said, 'A man likes some peace and quiet when he comes home. He likes his meal on the table.'

His comment was so left-field, I assumed he projected his own situation onto ours, or else his comment was based on some skewhiff belief that Thomas had given him as an excuse for what he did. Either way, these words were a shock. So, it was my fault – again. Did this friend, whom I considered a hero, realise I was standing there shaking and struggling to keep a grip on reality? A short time ago, I thought my daughter might've been dead.

Here was another misguided person, so typical of what I'd worn over the years. My reaction to the familiarity of his criticism was by now well practised. I took some deep breaths from the belly button, counted backwards from ten, to deal with the negative impressions served out to me by Thomas and his friends. It was all part of being in a couple front, and, in spite of this man's unnecessary and poorly timed advice, I was still grateful to him for his logical quick thinking. I thanked him once again and led him to the front door.

Later, when Thomas came out to have his dinner, he said in front of the children, as if he was the hero in this scenario, 'I was going to drive into the water but I couldn't do it.'

I hoped Becca was too young to understand the weight of what her father had just said. He, the perceived family man, sat down and shared dinner with his supposed loved ones.

The terror of the afternoon emptied me of all words as we ate our evening meal. That disclosure about the water and Thomas's intent put me on even higher alert. I was in a perpetual whirlpool of adrenaline and exhaustion, tuned to react to the slightest change in vibration. The simplest thing, such as making a cup of tea or hanging out the washing without Thomas in sight, felt like I was on a tightrope without a safety net. I needed to know Becca's movements every second of every day. I could see she had become his most valuable asset; the means to checkmate.

It seemed like divine intervention when during this difficult time I heard there was going to be an interview with a formerly married closet gay man on the radio. I'd searched our library and bought magazines looking for information which would help me understand more about my situation. It was rare to hear such a guest being interviewed.

I wanted to hear every word so before the broadcast I took the phone off the hook, got a notepad and pen and sat down to listen and take note. It became a case of taking note of his every shocking word. Here are some extracts:

Q: Why did you marry if you knew you were gay?

A: I thought that if I got married, it might stop me being gay. But, if it didn't, I could keep on doing what I usually did. I was used to that.

Q: Did you go out with girls?

A: Yes. Some.

Q: What was it about your wife?

A: She was attractive and friendly. I genuinely liked her. She was the perfect cover than if I'd chosen someone less attractive and less feminine.

Q: How's that?

A: Attractive women have more men around them and that was good for me.

My jaw dropped. His honesty shocked me.

A: I put a lot of thought into who'd be, I supposed you'd say, the best target.

Target. He said target. I recoiled.

A: I was desperate to hide my sexual identity. I'd grown up knowing how to hide it, but everyone was pressuring me to marry.

I knew this man. He sounded just like the one I'd married, the only difference being that this one was speaking some truth.

Q: What about your wife? Did you think she suffered?

A: I never thought that far ahead. It wasn't until she kept complaining about our lack of togetherness – that sort of thing – that made it harder.

Q: For you or for her?

A: Both, I suppose.

I wanted to shout at him. When was he ever going to admit that his wife suffered, and she suffered because of him; because of his lies, his deceit. Had he apologised to her for trashing her trust, love and fruitful years?

Q: We do know that, today, a woman living with a closet gay man is now in one of the highest risk groups for AIDS. Did you ever stop to think about the risks to your wife?

A: AIDS wasn't around when we married. I've never caught anything. I'm very careful.

My heart pumped too fast. This was all about him. For me, it was about having been someone's target. This guy seemed too preposterous to be real but the more he spoke, the more I believed him, and the more worthless I felt.

Q: Did you ever 'come out' to your wife?
A: Yes, eventually. We talked our way through it. We didn't want the children to suffer. We decided to go our separate ways and we've stayed friends.

I doubted Thomas would ever come out. I'd always hoped he would. It would make life so much easier. I was shocked and angered by this guy's candid answers. At the same time, I was thankful for RN and him shining a spotlight on such a dark place.

His revelations actually made me stronger, better informed, and gave me an inside run.

With a degree of better understanding, and some hope, I approached Thomas, one more time, about counselling. 'How would you feel about coming to counselling with me?'

'What for?'

'To talk about things. It'd be very low-key.'

To my surprise, he said, 'Okay.'

I organised an urgent appointment.

On the morning of the joint counselling session, Paul had already left to catch the bus to school. Becca was dressed ready for preschool. I found Thomas hovering in the hallway at the top of the internal stairs. He looked odd standing there in his old flannelette checked shirt, a pair of faded blue jeans and a pair of dirty old garden shoes. He'd seriously dressed down for the appointment, which seemed odd.

I said, 'You haven't had your breakfast or shower yet. Do you want me to drop Becca off then come back and get you?'

'I don't need breakfast. I don't need a shower.' He looked at me sideways then walked down the stairs and closed the bottom door.

These weird incongruities – his inappropriate old gardening clothes, his ultra cool manner when I expected him to be edgy, his apparent confidence meant he was up to something. My gut screamed. Not again. We were about to go to counselling.

I cleared up the last of the breakfast things, checked the car keys were in my pocket and called for Becca to come. I'd take her to preschool and come back for Thomas. If he didn't want to come he didn't have to. I'd go by myself, but there was still time to come back and pick him up if that's what he wanted.

Suddenly, I heard a dog yelping in the background. It sounded like it had been hit by a car. It was an unearthly sound. I wondered whose dog it was? The sound grew louder.

I raced out the back door because the sound seemed to be coming up our side passage. I rushed to the side gate only to see it wasn't an injured animal. It was Thomas yelping with flames leaping from his collar, cuffs and ankles.

It was unbelievable. My thoughts were to get him to the ground – get him to the ground – roll him over, but when I opened the gate he ran at me then past me towards the lawn.

I yelled, 'Get to the hose, get to the hose.'

I had to stop Becca from coming out. She'd come to the door and could see it was her father yelping and alight.

I gathered her up and raced her into the bedroom, kissed her on the crown of her head and said, 'Mummy wants you to stay here. Daddy had an accident. Here's a Care Bear - can you play with your Care Bears? Yes?'

I put her favourite Care Bear into her arms. 'Stay here, darling. I'll be back. Okay.'

I turned on her bedroom light, left her hugging Care Bear and closed the door but it couldn't shut out the piercing screams. Then I raced out to Thomas, who had reached the hose but had fallen onto the ground before he could turn it on. He was in too much agony to function.

I didn't want to hurt him, but had to roll him over. 'I'm sorry, I'm sorry,' I said as I rolled him on the grass in an attempt to put out the flames with the hose.

By that time, he was in another state of consciousness and soaking wet.

'Thomas - I have to ring for an ambulance.'

He was beyond; out of range of sense and sound.

'I'm ringing an ambulance.'

I raced inside and dialled 000. I shook so much it hurt to keep still. I stated the emergency.

The lady said, '... take him to the shower... the paramedics are on their way... I'll stay on the phone - come back when you can.'

'Okay.'

I flew out. Sprayed another soft spray of water over him and watched skin peel back on one of his heels. The layers were tissue paper thin and whitest nearest the bone. I desperately needed to stop watching this horror.

'Thomas - the shower - I have to get you to the shower. An ambulance is coming. C'mon.'

Thomas was impossibly heavy.

I said, 'I'm sorry but I have to do this.'

I started to lift him. He screamed and screamed. He was bigger than me, but I had to get him to the shower.

'Thomas - the shower. Help me. You have to help me.'

My desperation gave me a strength I didn't know I had. With all the company of heaven, I coaxed him down the few back steps onto the pavers. We struggled to stay upright. When we reached the bathroom, I turned on the shower just enough to keep him wet and ran to get him a chair.

I called out, 'You'll be okay. You'll be okay.'

His screams curled into deep harrowing moans. They echoed through the house. As I put him onto the chair and ran the shower, I heard a siren; a brilliant sound. I raced to the front door and the paramedics hurried in and took over.

Most of the neighbours were at work but one neighbour from across the road was home and she came to the front door and called out, 'Can I be of any help?'

An angel. I asked if she could take Becca. Becca liked Mrs E. When I brought her out of the bedroom, Becca looked a picture of innocence with her Care Bear and standing there in her Punky Brewster outfit with Punky Brewster plaits all ready for preschool. I gave her a big hug and said, 'Darling, can you go with Mrs. E, please? Daddy's okay but he needs to go to hospital.'

I hurried to the phone and the very kind lady was still there. As she spoke to me, all I could do was cry. As I shook, I didn't believe it was possible to shake this hard and not break any bones.

In the background, I heard paramedics talking to Thomas. One of them had a deep soothing voice, just like my Dad's.

The lady on the phone said, 'Do you have a relative you can call?'

'No. I don't live near family.'

'Which one lives closest?'

'My brother.'

'You're going to need someone like him, a relative, to be with you today, so please ring them.'

I heard Thomas tell the paramedics that he'd gone down to mow the lawn and when he was filling the mower with petrol, it must've caught alight. I was stunned that he couldn't tell the truth, even now, with his life at stake but I supposed it was a pre-planned story.

I can't remember how I met up with my sister-in-law, Robyn, that day. We sat in a coffee shop just down from the hospital. I was so grateful for her being there, for leaving her extended care unit which she ran at Wyong Hospital, to come and sit with a very messed-up me.

After she left, I drove home and with heartfelt thanks I picked up Becca from Mrs E. The children and I had afternoon tea and Becca told Paul her version of what had happened. Later, I told Paul more about the petrol and the accident.

'Mum, you know Dad. It wouldn't have been an accident.'

'I know,' and we hugged.

It wasn't fair that we had to go through this but, as our former Prime Minister, Malcolm Fraser, once said, 'Life wasn't meant to be easy.'

We knew that.

# The Social Worker

Thomas was taken by ambulance from the Royal Newcastle Hospital to the Burns unit at Royal North Shore (RNS), St Leonards. He had burns to thirty-five percent of his body.

The doctor said, "It's touch and go. We don't know yet which way it'll go.'

Thank heavens for automaticity. It kept me breathing and my heart beating. I'd known instinctively what to do for his body at the time but, at this moment, I didn't know what to do for mine. My ears still reverberated with the inhumanity of his screams and howls. The very core of my being pared off into illogical, incomprehensible images of conflagration, beyond anything I'd seen.

I looked down as if from above. I relied on my roots to stay grounded, like the Liquidamber out the front. I needed to be like her and mimic the brave way her branches accommodated even the wildest of winds.

It was 10 o'clock at night, Thomas's witching hour, when the phone rang. He'd been in hospital three days. I'd imagined him bandaged to the 'nth degree and highly drugged and in dreamland but I heard, 'Hello, sweetheart. I pulled it off.'

He sounded bright. 'Thomas? What?'

'I pulled it off.'

'Pulled what off?'

'The painting. I changed it over and they're none the wiser.'

'What painting?'

'The one in this room. You know the one I told you about. I couldn't stand the one that was in here. I've swapped them.' And he laughed.

This was not the image I had of Thomas in hospital. Did he know he was on the literal verge of living or dying?

'Should you be moving around like that? I mean, how did you –the tubes –?'

'No one saw me.'

'Aren't you all tied up with tubes?'

'I can walk with them.'

'Are you walking already?'

Thomas was at death's door and his main aim was to exchange paintings, in adjoining rooms, without staff seeing him. That's why he was so excited. It had been a challenge to the sixty-five percent of his body that hadn't been burnt. He knew he was on 24/7 watch and it proved to him that he could still do things without anyone seeing him. He sounded proud of his achievement.

'There's no one around when they do changeovers.'

Later that night, I rang the hospital. I told them what he'd done and how he'd been a schedules clerk and was aware of their scheduling.

'Don't worry,' the night nurse said. 'He's hallucinating. There's no way he could've done that.'

'But, he's capable of doing whatever he sets his mind to. He told me yesterday he was going to try and swap them.'

'As far as I know, he hasn't left his bed but I'll look into it. Now, you go and have a good night's sleep and stop worrying.'

To their credit, staff checked on the paintings. And, yes, the pictures had been swapped.

Thomas's psychiatrist rang me early next morning. 'When can you come down and see me?'

I was working, and had two children to look after, but angels – that is, my dear friends and neighbours, helped out with the children. In the meantime, shift times were changed and I travelled down early next morning. Thomas was unaware of my visit.

My consultation with his psychiatrist lasted an hour and a half. Somehow, he condensed the past seventeen years of my life with Thomas into ninety minutes. Considering he hadn't lived with us, he must've been the proverbial fly on the wall.

'And he... '

'Yes.'

'And he... '

'Yes.'

'A textbook case.'

'Really?'

So, my husband of seventeen years was a textbook case. The happenings, the ones I'd been living with, were in a textbook.

'You mean to say other people do these things?'

'Yes.'

I felt a rush of relief. So it wasn't just me, like Thomas had said. I was hardly game to ask, 'What happens next?'

'You have to get the best lawyer you can. No ordinary lawyer. You need someone who'll scare the daylights out of him should he consider making a wrong move. He needs to know he could go to jail.'

My heart pounded. I tried to breathe deeply but felt there wasn't enough air in the room for the two of us.

'Will he improve? Can he get better?'

'He's reached this age without intervention. That's not good. There are medications but he has to be prepared to take them.'

'He never takes the ones the other psychiatrist gave him. He'd read up on their side effects before his appointment and would pretend he had them. He thought it was funny.'

'Unfortunately, the people who need antipsychotics are often the very ones who don't take them. Some of the medications have unpleasant side effects... if he decides to take them, he could lead a normal life.'

I told him about Thomas's closet gayness. I thought that was his biggest problem. 'I've always made allowances for him because I felt sorry for him.'

'Don't worry. This is not about that. He might never come out.'

'I don't understand.'

'It's not about that. This is about control. You have to find a good lawyer who's prepared to throw the book at him. Ring the Law Society and tell them what I've said. They'll have an idea who to recommend. We'll look after him here – you go and look after yourself and the children.'

That night, Thomas rang at ten p.m. upset. 'They've changed my cutlery.'

"What do you mean?'

'They've given me plastic. They expect me to eat with plastic. They're up to something. I know because they're messing with the shifts.'

After a couple of weeks, I was advised to take the children to see their father, a terrible suggestion made by his social worker.

Thomas said, 'She'd like to meet you. You'll like her. She's a lovely woman.'

I hid my amusement when I first met her. She'd pulled her chair up close to Thomas's bed. She lent forward as she spoke to him. The top buttons of her ochre-coloured silken blouse were undone in a revealing way.

She turned to me with puppy eyes and said, 'Thomas is such a beautiful man.'

She was smitten and she wasn't the first. Over the years, many women flirted with Thomas. He never discouraged them because I could see how the attention flattered and amused him. I was often tempted to lean across and say to the keen ones, 'You're wasting your time.'

The social worker's reasoning was that the children needed to see their father to stop them from imagining something worse than it was. Becca didn't want to go in. I was relieved. Paul and I went in and it was worse for our son than anything a child could ever imagine. The smell of burnt flesh was like no other.

When we walked out, Paul said, 'Mum, you won't let me watch horror movies. This is worse than any horror movie.'

'I know. It's the pits. I'm sorry, I'm so sorry you had to go through that. You won't again. After this, you can watch as many horror movies as you like.'

We laughed; laughter straight out of a bad horror movie.

I spoke to a nurse and said we had to go. Her nod was full of compassion. I didn't take the children back to the hospital again. They sent their father cards and rang him instead.

I procured a lawyer; a senior partner with Clayton Utz. He'd been a former Family Law Court judge, ironically enough in Newcastle. It had become painful and dangerous for us to stay trapped in Thomas's games, some of which could've taken our lives. I couldn't decipher what drove him - was it personality, character, illness? For everyone's sake, I had to stop thinking, and leave, regardless of what drove him. It would be taking the greater risk.

Sitting alone in the solicitor's office added to my feelings of shame. I'd hidden a lot from others out of shame and pride. I didn't want our family to be the subject of gossip. I had to protect the children. I worried that if I spoke out, other than to a couple of close friends, it might be too heavy to hear and besides who'd believe me? I hardly believed it myself.

A junior solicitor was assigned to me as a money-saver. She was a former high school teacher and loved the law. It took all day to prepare the affidavit and she drank so many cans of Coke during the day, that I said, 'You could get an ulcer if you keep drinking Coke like that. I used to clean my china painting brushes in Coke and it stripped them squeaky clean.'

She laughed. 'With a story like yours, you're lucky I'm only drinking Coke.'

# A Reasonable Man

It was time for my ten-year check-up. As I lay on the bed in the MRI tunnel, the radiographer came out and called through the tunnel, 'Where was the bleed?'

'In the brainstem.'

'We can only find a small crystal in there.'

The MRI showed uninterrupted blood flow. No malformation except for the small crystal. Ten years earlier, the malformation was the size of a thumbnail. At the time, my neurologist had said, 'Sometimes miracles happen. Things can shrink or seal themselves off and the blood is re routed. Think of it as a time bomb... main thing is to avoid stress or athletic sex.'

I laughed, but he didn't.

'We don't want it flexing again.'

With such good news, I wanted to sing and dance and have athletic sex. No, I'm joking about the sex. Singing and dancing would be more than enough. 'That's wonderful news. I can't believe it.'

'It's hard to see what's going on in that part of the brain but it's looking better than a few years ago.'

'Thank you so much.'

Dr. T sat back in his chair and said, "Well, Anne, I hope not to see you again, at least, not under these circumstances. Whatever you're doing, keep doing it.'

I smiled and thought, if only you knew. It must've been the bucketloads of athletic stress that contributed.

Sadly, around this time, my eldest brother, Robert, died suddenly.

It was a terrible shock. He had been the elite athlete in the family and an athletic's coach outside of work. His young daughters were also shining athletes. Robert's sudden death would be the first of a cluster of significant deaths on both sides of our family for the next twelve months.

Thomas and my separation was a kind of death. It involved loss and grief; a crumbling of dreams and a trashing of hope. Even so, the children and I continued to meet up with him. I assumed now that he lived, and had settled into his role as the official caretaker, at a fledgling museum - a legend in his own right on the rail enthusiasts' stage – that he'd be more grounded.

As there'd been no frightening episodes during the past year, we planned Christmas activities in Sydney. Our parents lived a few kilometres apart. While Family Law had made me the official supervisor when Thomas was with the children, I no longer had fears because we'd shared so many happy family birthdays, special occasions, all without incident. Sometimes, we visited Thomas at the rail museum, where he proudly showed us the restoration work on the old rail motor carriages.

We planned with his mother, June, that she and Thomas would take the children for a day out to Taronga Zoo after Christmas. June would be the unofficial supervisor; a slight relaxation of orders.

On that day, my extended family had planned a post-Christmas lunch-dinner at my cousin's place. I would've liked the children to have been there but, as they'd be the only children going, I agreed they'd probably enjoy going to the zoo with Nanny Train and Dad more, as both children were crazy about animals.

Both Thomas and June agreed, 'It'll be nice for you to catch up with your family. It's been a hard year for you.'

At my cousin's place, we sat around the table and talked and laughed but behind my laughter was an unease which I tried to reason away. Of course, I'd feel like this. We didn't have mobile phones back then, so I had to wait until we got home before I could ring the children and see what sort of day they'd had. I knew that once I heard their voices, my anxiety, which had knotted my stomach to the point where I couldn't eat or drink, would ease. I struggled to focus on the moment with extended family. I'd laugh when they laughed, not too sure what I was laughing about. As a family, we'd had such a tough year that it was good to hear everyone relaxing and telling old tales about this one and that.

I tried to convince myself that all was well with the children but my gut knew otherwise. Thomas's history sat heavily on my shoulders and I inwardly begged to leave.

On the drive home, Mum said to me, 'You're very quiet.'

'I have a bad feeling.'

'That's understandable. You just wait and see. They'll have had a great time. You'll learn one day that worry gets you nowhere.'

When we finally arrived home, Dad drove up the driveway. Mum reached the back door first. She bent down and picked up something while Dad went around to the front and came through the house, putting lights on and unlocking the back door.

Mum said, 'What's this?'

I stood at the end of the family queue. It was too dark to see what she was talking about. By the time I'd walked inside, Mum had unpinned a note attached to a bouquet of red roses.

'Oh,' she said, 'it's for you,' and she handed me the roses and envelope.

I saw Thomas's immaculate 'Anne' written in large flourished letters across the front of the envelope.

I opened it and read the unthinkable. He wouldn't. He wouldn't.

Dad put the kettle on and Mum sat down.

She said, 'Well?'

I didn't know which part to read aloud. I said, 'It's Thomas. He's taken the children to-'

'Where to?'

'I don't know – to his place, I think.' I didn't tell them he'd actually written a goodbye letter and I quote, 'By the time you read this, the children will be in heaven... I'll meet them soon... you can start a new life... we won't be in your way.'

It was unbelievable. I was in his horror movie again. It couldn't be. I'd been filled with such hope. I rang June.

'Hi, Nan, may I speak to Paul, please?'

'He's not here, Darling.'

I shivered. Felt faint. Every second counted but I knew Nanny could be easily tipped. I had to be careful.

'Do you know where he is?'

'I thought you knew.'

'I was going to pick them up in the morning, remember?'

'Why? What's the matter?'

'Did Thomas say anything before he left?'

'Not really.'

'How was he when you were at the zoo?'

'I didn't go. I wasn't feeling well but they said they had a nice time. Look, Darling, I thought you knew. He said the plans had been changed.'

'No.'

This was all my fault. I should've made it clearer to June how important it was to keep the children in her sight.

I said, 'I'm sure they'll be fine but he wasn't meant to take them.'

'I think he said they were going to his place. I don't know. I'm sorry. I'm not sure.'

I had to get off the phone, tell my parents and ring the police. I read some of the letter to the policeman and gave him some history but I could tell he doubted me. I said, 'If you ring the hospital, they'll have records.'

'Where do you think he is?'

'He could've taken them to where he lives. I don't know. He's not supposed to have taken them, so it's hard to say.'

A gravelly voice in the background said, 'Yeah, he's probably got them for the Christmas holidays and she's causing trouble.'

I was astounded. I wanted to yell down the line to the cynic, 'If only my life was that simple.'

'I'm sorry I can't tell you where he is. There's a mate who lives opposite his place. I'll ring him and see if he can see any lights.'

I rang another of Thomas's friends to get the number, rang the guy then rang the police with some relief. 'Yes. There are lights on and his car's there.'

Could Thomas really- ? I had to pray that the self in him that had fainted during *Bonnie and Clyde* would be the same self who couldn't, wouldn't, harm his children.

The southern police rang the northern police. The ones up north said they couldn't do anything until the southern station had sighted the alleged letter, and the letter needed to be confirmed by someone other than the wife. And they needed to know from someone, other than the wife, if the letter was in the father's handwriting.

I gave the police his mother's phone number. She confirmed he'd written something, which appeared to be a letter, before he left with the children. She confirmed that the children were meant to go back to the mother the next day but her son had told her that the plans had been changed.

The southern police satisfied the northern police, who then headed out to the village; to the train museum situated behind a strip of shops; a quiet spot.

Paul told me later that when the police arrived, he and Becca were watching a video in one carriage and his father was somewhere else. 'It was like in the movies. The police rammed their way in - they took us out to the ambulance and some of them went to find Dad.'

I was relieved when I heard that the police had taken every precaution to look after the children. They rang me immediately to tell me the children were safe; that they'd been fully checked. Becca spoke on the phone but she didn't say much.

I told her, 'I'll be there soon, darling. I'm coming up now. Love you.'

Paul spoke as if he had the situation in hand. I was angry that this was too much for any fifteen year-old to handle.

'Mum, I'd better go with Dad.'

'What do you mean?'

'Dad's got to go in the paddy wagon by himself.'

'You can't go in that. Stay with Becca, please.'

'No, she's fine. She's got a really nice policewoman looking after her. I'd better go with Dad and check he's ok.'

'He'll be fine, Darling.'

'Just to be sure, Mum.'

'I don't want you to -'

'It's cool, Mum. Don't worry.'

Paul knew nothing about the letter and he'd become an expert at parenting his father, something I never wanted to see, for any child.

Before they got into the paddy wagon, Paul said, 'Dad told them we were having a holiday with him.'

And he assumed that what his Dad said must be right. On the drive to the police station in the paddy wagon, Paul said he overheard the policemen talking.

'He doesn't seem like much trouble.'

'He seems pretty reasonable to me.'

# Faultlines

The police rang me later that night.

'He's been taken to the Mental Health Unit for assessment.'

'Thank you, so much.'

When I rang the hospital, they suggested ringing back in the morning because they didn't know when Thomas would see the doctor. 'There's quite a queue.'

I rang the hospital the next morning, before we left for Sydney to attend Nanna Rose's funeral.

The receptionist said, 'He went home last night.'

'Oh, I thought he might've been admitted for a couple of days.'

'Apparently not.'

Why was I surprised? A wave of fear rushed over me. My balance tipped. Of course, I should've known. Thomas would've been perfectly cooperative and would've seemed perfectly reasonable. His way around the truth was his second skin.

Fortunately, the police must've had second thoughts because they rang me two days later and advised me to take out an AVO, asap. I rang my solicitor. It seemed a terribly cruel thing to do but it had to be done.

The day after the abduction was our grandmother, Nana Rose's funeral. It was 28 December 1989. We left Newcastle and headed back to Sydney. About half an hour out of Newcastle, south of Swansea, we felt a strong shudder in the car. Sirens and more sirens, ambulances and fire engines soon roared past us heading north towards Newcastle.

The announcer on the radio interrupted the program to say, '... ten thirty a.m... a 5.6 Richter magnitude earthquake...'

The earthquake was far worse than expected. More than 160 people were injured and, tragically, thirteen people died. It was to be our nation's worst earthquake.

The children and I seemed to be in the midst of so much trauma. For now, we had to put the news and my concerns about the earthquake and our house on the back-burner.

Christmas had been sad because of the loved ones who were no longer talking and laughing with us. Also now, we were doubly sad because Nanna Rose had died. We went to her funeral but I have no memory of it. I remember being at the wake afterwards at Pat and Roy's place where we celebrated Nanna Rose's long life.

It was lovely to be there, wrapped up in a warm family group. We stood there in the middle of normalcy. It was comforting to know that life went on. I couldn't wait, though, to get back to 39 and ring around and find out from my neighbours if they were okay and to see if our house was still standing.

Once back at 39, I tried to ring neighbours on either side but their phone lines were down. The TV news showed utter devastation; widespread damage to buildings and houses; many of which I recognised - some too close to home - and tragically there was the awful loss of life.

I couldn't help but make a metaphoric link between the earth's fault line and ours. Our personal seismic waves had proved too much for the earth. I tried to put the past twenty-four hours out of my mind when persistent what-ifs broke through. What if -? What if he'd -? I hadn't yet had time to clear my mind.

Mostly, I was annoyed with myself. How could I have been so easily lulled into a false sense of security? Would Thomas's horror movie never end? I knew it was payback but, surely, he could see what he was doing to our children?

The day after Nana Rose's funeral, the background in the living room at 39 was surreal. The cheer squad oohed and arghed at the TV whenever an Australian cricketer hit a four or a six. They gasped and roared when the batsman was caught or bowled out. You would've thought someone had died. Meanwhile, I sat in the kitchen with Dad and the children while the TV replayed the tragedy of fallen wickets.

I wanted to cry. A potential family tragedy had almost unfolded in our laps; an emotional earthquake had hit us, and, as yet, no one had asked us if we were okay or given us a hug. I understood. We were in the too hard basket. No-one really knew what to say. I also suspected that no-one wanted to risk opening the emotional floodgates with hugs and sympathy.

On the news, we heard that billions of dollars' worth of damage had been done during the earthquake and an estimated 35,000 homes were damaged. The cheering squad didn't want to hear about my concerns that our home might've been damaged.

After lunch, I rang my neighbour on the southern side. Her phone was working.

She said, 'When it happened we were sitting outside on the upstairs balcony having morning tea. We were counting the line of cold ships out to sea, when suddenly the house rolled forward. For a second, I thought we were going to fall off then it rolled back and we heard this almighty crack. D said, I bet he's (Thomas) planted a bloody bomb.'

Fortunately not. It was the sound of our brick house cracking diagonally from front to back.

I rang our neighbours on the other side, the northern side.

Jane said, '... it was my birthday. Peter and I were at the shopping centre when suddenly the building started shaking and groaning... it was like a weird metallic, grinding sound... my sister had to evacuate patients into the park next to the hospital... some people coming out of anaesthetic woke up under a blue sky. They wondered if they'd gone to the afterlife... The good news is the power's back on. Now, how about you? How are you?'

I nearly burst into tears.

Someone had said, 'How are you?'

This was the first time anyone had asked me how I was since the terror-filled night when I thought I'd lost my children and blamed myself for being so gullible. I had no idea how I was, so I faked an answer.

She said, 'Peter's been over and checked your place. He said there's some damage but not to worry. It's nothing serious.'

That was an incredible relief but I needed to see it. It was time to cut our intended holiday in Sydney short and head for home. I hung up and walked out to the living room just as another Australian cricketer was bowled out. Cries went up.

'Oh, no!'

'He's out, oh no!'

'That's terrible. Oh, no. He's out.'

No one could take their eyes off the horror being replayed on the screen.

I turned back and went in and rang June.

Her voice crackled. As expected, she was upset. She coughed and sounded breathless. She whispered, 'I'm sorry, darling. I can't talk. I can't say anything, really. He's my son. You know what he's like.' Her voice was paper-thin. 'If anything had happened, I'd never have forgiven myself.'

'I know. You take care.'

We said 'I love you' and hung up.

Paul and Becca had settled almost permanently beside Poppy, who sat at the head of the table in the kitchen, in a chronic unwell state with his ventilator as constant companion on one side, and usually Mum, his other constant companion, sitting on the other side except when the cricket was on.

I said to the children, 'We'll be off now, off home, so say goodbye to everyone.'

Dad frowned and Mum looked surprised.

'Are you sure?' Mum said.

'Yes. I need to get home and deal with the damage.'

The children look relieved. The holiday-makers looked relieved. And, I was relieved. I wouldn't have to keep up a pretence that everything was honky-dory-holiday-mode.

On the way home, Paul said, 'Mum, when we came back from Dad's, you know, no one asked if we were ok?'

'Didn't they? They didn't ask me either. I apologise for that. I'm sorry. And how are you?'

'Okay, and you?'

'Yes, I'm okay. Thanks for asking, Darling.'

It was an enormous relief when we turned into our driveway. Everyone was pleased to be home. The large crack out the front was under the main bedroom window. Our neighbour explained how the earthquake had been an east-west roll, which is why the brick walls split diagonally, front to back.

The inside of the house had hairline cracks at stress points in corners and joints. Strains ruptured and bled into gyprock and plaster. Pictures hung askew. The house looked exactly like how I felt. The dazed, shocked city mirrored my liminal state situated somewhere between damage and recovery.

It would be twelve months before all the damage was fixed. I had the inside of the house repainted and new carpet laid then put the house on the market. I needed to buy a smaller home; one with a tiny loan. We had to leave behind our magical outlook and wonderful neighbours. While the house was fully restored, repairs to our family well-being would take much longer.

Many people who'd experienced separation said, 'Give yourself a good four years before it gets better,' and so it was.

The children recalibrated in their own way. Becca, ten years younger than Paul, had become withdrawn. It was important for me to role-play with her every day. We'd sit on the sunroom floor where she surrounded herself with Lego, Care Bears and ponies of every description. Becca led the storylines. I was her echo. In those weeks, Becca's stories were about healing many injured animals. They were taken to the vet hospital and made better. In later years, she'd became a veterinary nurse, amongst other things.

On the social and emotional side, our family was fortunate to have angels, like Jane and Peter next door. They were as important to us as fresh air. Their youngest, Chris, was six months younger than Becca. He was a lively funny boy. He and Becca were great friends. They played together, went to preschool together; essential stability, security and fun.

As Becca grew older, she learnt ballet, tap dancing and pottery, and had swimming lessons, all of which gave her enjoyment and renewed confidence and flipped her fear.

Paul continued to play guitar, wrote and sang songs and read fantasy novels. He loved being in the bush checking out geckos and water dragons, down at the Falls, with his friends. He also surfed.

One day, he came racing into the kitchen, his body alight with energy. He stood there with his surfboard as witness. 'Mum, guess what? I saw God this morning.'

'Really. Where?'

'In the waves. God's in the sun - he's the light - he shone through the spray. He's in everything. He is everything.'

'That's amazing, darling,' and, of course, I believed him. I could see God in my son's dazzling eyes and I heard God in his awe.

Months after Thomas moved out and the children and I were sitting at the table in the sunroom eating dinner, Paul said, 'You know, Mum, this is better.'

'The meal?'

'No. It's better without Dad being upset all the time.'

'You think so?'

'It's sad - it's very sad but it's better. It'll be better for him, too. He can be with his mates.'

'Yes. Hopefully, this is better for everyone.'

Previously, Paul had come to me and said, "Dad's gay, isn't he?"

'Yes.'

'Don't tell him I know. He'll be embarrassed. Leave it like it is. He can tell me when he's ready.'

And he did, almost a decade later.

At that time, I believed his father would probably never be ready. He was still in denial and that was a problem. Living with, and in and around, his secret had become increasingly difficult. I noticed that once he reached his mid-forties his private and public selves merged. He'd noticeably became more of who he needed to be. At least, now he could live with his tribe and with purpose. I didn't envy them, should he get upset with one of them.

Years later, Becca would say, 'Some of my friends were badly affected by their parents' divorce but yours didn't really affect me.'

'Really? Why not?'

'I think because their parents still hate each other but you and Dad are good friends.'

# Afterword

*1993 Mount Victoria*

For days, weeks, months we lived in sheer relief, absorbing the healing power of peace. The children and I continued to have regular family outings with their father. Sometimes, we went to the pictures, ate popcorn, shared packets of Maltesers and drank fizzy drinks. We picnicked at Blackbutt Reserve, counted the swans, fed the birds, took photos, shared news.

It was usual for us to walk to the top of the reserve and visit the koalas and sit on picnic rugs and eat salad rolls and peel mandarins. Those family outings became the best of times. They proved to be an important investment in the well-being of our newly adapted family unit.

One afternoon when the picnic was over and fold-up chairs were being packed into the boot of the car, Thomas doubled over. 'I feel funny.'

I thought, here we go, but this was no fake scene. He looked grey, was breathless and could hardly speak. '... bricks on my chest.'

We raced to the family GP, who was only a few kilometres away, and within days Thomas had open heart surgery. It gave him a whole new lease of life.

The children and I enjoyed our new life, too. While the budget was tight, we had a solid roof over our heads, made yummy sandwiches, packed nibblies and fruit drinks and went to the local park, to the beach or for a bushwalk down to Glenrock Lagoon. We could soak in nature: the ocean, the waterfalls, the creek, the birds, the geckos, the snakes, the wildflowers, the towering eucalypts and warm friendships. All were on our doorstep.

The sale of the family home went well and the children and I moved into the inner city. I bought a character-filled home built in the 1880s.

It was a stand-alone, two bedroom double brick in town. I had new plumbing and new wiring installed. 108 Dawson Street was so small I used to say, 'There's got to be a door here somewhere to the rest of the house but I can't seem to find it.'

We walked everywhere: to the beach, to the city centre, to parks, to art galleries, to the library, to sports centres and to shops, all in close proximity. While Paul was on a fifty per cent scholarship at Grammar, selling the house would help pay his school fees but he made the decision to leave and go to the local high school where he already had friends. There wasn't as much pressure on him to perform, which filled him with constant anxiety, on top of what he'd been living through.

Becca settled into the local primary school. She took to walking to school with the older girl next door.

I kept on part-time teaching and ran a small tutoring school. I sold articles and was halfway through a creative writing unit at uni. I'd previously finished and enriching year long volunteer guides' course, one day a week, at Newcastle Regional Art Gallery, run by the talented education officer, Sonya C. Those training days and tours given to high school students were my essential soul food.

I designed new gardens out the front and back of our house; hunted down nurseries which sold Victorian-era type cottage plants. We put in a Victorian era letterbox and a tall matching lamp. The only modern touch was the lamp's light sensor. I painted the old-fashioned front picket fence the same vintage dark green as the lamp. Borrowed a topiary book from the library and, guided by instructions, we trimmed the healthy lilly-pilly in the front garden into a ball. It thrived in the handkerchief of a garden which consisted of poor sandy soil. Becca and I built up the soil with newspapers and fallen leaves from the plane trees out the front and which filled the street's gutters.

Paul and his friends helped load up second-hand bricks into the station wagon and I had them professionally laid out the back in a large circle, with curved paths creating garden beds, in which we planted veggies and herbs. We also planted old-fashioned cottage plants out the front and back.

Paul and his friends built a modified skateboard ramp right down the back where, in the mid 1800s, stables once stood. A couple of fathers lent the boys tools and often called in to check the structural integrity of their work, for which I was very thankful.

I'd set my alarm early of a morning to complete uni assignments and/or prepare lessons. There was comfort in the early morning silence. I'd stop work once I heard hungry footsteps in the hallway and Paul calling out, 'Hey, Mum, what's for brekkie?'

'The usual - Weetbix.'

After Paul completed his HSC, he did a six months' hospitality TAFE course in preparation for his travels. He'd worked casual for a couple of years, after school and on weekends, in a busy city cafe. With his own money, he bought a lathe, surfboards and music equipment but soon he began to save in earnest. He wanted one day to go around Australia and, 'After that, I want to go around the world.'

With his savings and birthday money for his eighteenth birthday, he set off up north with a mate on a working trip around Australia. He was well prepared, capable and deserved to follow his dreams.

His first stop was to work on a macadamia farm where he met his life partner, Karen, and they would go on to have three beautiful sons. At first, they lived in a wood shack with a tent over the top. The valley they were in had magnificent views. Paul had been promised work in hospitality in Queensland but soon heard the business had been sold and the offer of work had fallen through. He found work on a banana plantation nearby and Karen found domestic work. We visited them in their beautiful setting. They lived simply and had moved into their own tent on the grounds of a macadamia farm which had a large weather shelter with barbecues, tables, and amenities. Their rent was to pick a hession sack of macadamias a week.

Thomas took a golden handshake twelve months after our property settlement. He retired at forty-five and settled into the quiet country town where he became the official caretaker of the rail museum. Once again, I could see how at home he was with his tribe. Now that he was financially comfortable, he planned overseas trips with his friends. There were signs of his original beauty coming back. He was definitely on the right track.

I continued with my studies. They were a lifeline. Whenever I completed an assignment or posted an article, I'd reward myself by walking around to Darby's, the local bakery, a block away. I'd buy, something like, two fresh cheese and onion buns and a caramel slice and a passionfruit tart. Back home, I'd boil the jug, make a cuppa and give myself a pat on the back. I'd learnt how to give myself metaphorical pats on the back.

While friends were a wonderful support, there were those vulnerable moments each day when it was up to me to give myself a pat on the back. 'Well done, girl. You did it. Keep going.'

As a single parent, lots of decisions in daily life are made up of a multitude of acute tummy-flipping moments. Such moments I liken to the tummy-flipping moment when you're about to be wheeled into the operating theatre and you know no one else can take your place. As a single parent, you wear many hats. I was the patient, surgeon and theatre nurse. I was also the sum of the team responsible for the outcome – good and bad.

Now was the perfect opportunity to follow my dream. I'd move to my beloved Blue Mountains where I'd once owned land. Becca and I enjoyed inner-city life but the image of my beloved mountains was always at the back of my mind. I'd promised myself that one day I'd live there, if I could.

Before that decision, and for the past two years, I'd blocked out three consecutive days a month in my diary. The *hyggleig* retreat always required planning and preparation. I'd clear all appointments/commitments and divert all phone calls to the answering machine. Becca and I would go to the shops and choose food. We'd go to the library and my cherub would choose her favourite books, videos and crafts. We stayed in our pj's during our respite, if we wanted. We set up mini feasts and chilled out for the entire weekend.

Becca had to go to school on the last of the three days, so she was classed as a two-day-*hyggleig* girl. In contrast to how I'd felt three days earlier, by mid-Monday anything was possible.

Considering what us girls had been through, we needed to burrow deep. We needed longer walks in nature. We needed to dance to Abba and Atwell's honky-tonk; to conduct Clayderman and soar with Galway; to go indigo deep with Chopin's nocturnes while taking long candlelit baths.

I had no idea when the move would happen but it was on its way. I just had to wait. I hadn't decided exactly where I wanted to live in the mountains. I needed to buy in a village which had a primary school close to home. If my car ever broke down, I'd need public transport. We needed a general store or something similar and ideally a post office.

The move came when I least expected it. I was working mid morning at my desk by the back door where the light was strongest. I listened to the background hum of traffic a block away. I heard the steady murmur of M's voice next door talking to a friend on the phone. The warmth of the sun on my back was kind. I gazed back into the house towards the living room thinking about nothing in particular.

That's when I saw a grey wispy form float towards me. As it drifted past I felt a slight breeze. My immediate thought was, 'That's Death.' I don't know why but it left me with a knowledge that it was time to go.

I needed to respect the importance of my decision so I headed for Darby's. This was the perfect occasion to lash out and buy two freshly baked onion and Vegemite rolls, two pineapple tarts, a caramel slice and a small carton of strawberry milk.

As I turned the corner, I caught up with a young couple who'd stopped on the footpath in front of me to read a real estate brochure. As I walked past, we all smiled and said hello. They reminded me so much of Thomas and myself over twenty years ago. As I walked on, I sent them a silent prayer in case they needed it.

It was time to test my resolve. I needed to spend some time in the mountains and see if it was possible to follow my dream. It was midwinter when Becca and I booked into a guest house at Wentworth Falls. We spent time exploring the villages that were on my wishlist. I had no idea that I'd buy an almost completed brand-new two-bedroom fire resistant timber townhouse in beautiful Mount Victoria.

The day Becca and I looked at it, there was mist everywhere. There'd been heavy rain and we couldn't see into the distant mountains and valleys but I knew they were there and this was it. I put our Newcastle house on the market and it sold immediately.

I could rave on about the special features of 55A Victoria St, built by a former monk. Its harmonious Feng Shui elements were special. At certain times of the year, the sun rose in an upstairs eastern window and set in the western side of the bedroom/study. No rainforest timbers were used in the build. It had views from every window which added up to a 360° perspective overall. The back faced due north.

The village itself was more than I dreamed possible. The primary school was next door to our house. Becca made a lovely lifelong friend on her first day at school. When she brought her new-found friend home after school to see if she could play, it turned out that her mother happened to be the very person's name I'd been given by someone at my last meeting with the Fellowship of Australian writers in Newcastle. Penny's name was the only contact number I had in this village of 900 people. Like our daughters, our first meeting seeded a lifelong friendship and we soon became each other's extended family.

To reach the general store and post office, we walked through the school grounds next door. It was used by locals as common ground. The railway station was further down, easy walking distance. On my wish list I'd forgotten to ask for a bookstore. I needn't have worried. Mount Victoria boasted two excellent second-hand ones. There were cosy eateries and a delightful old picture theatre, Mt Vic Flicks, which ran both popular and art house movies.

Becca and I loved our afternoon walks. Pulpit Rock and Sunset Rock Lookouts were only minutes away. At times, the frosty chill nipped our noses and our cheeks fired apple-red. On our walks home, we'd swing our arms to keep warm. We'd watch Mount Charles settle down for the night under the sinking sun. Its golden afternoon rays blessed waratah and wattle. On the apple tree outside the kitchen window, expectant buds shed their winter fur coats in readiness for spring.

# Acknowledgements

I spent the first 30 years of my life in a tree-lined conservative evangelical belt, on the top of a ridge, on the northern side of Sydney Harbour, where the Pacific Highway followed ancient wallaby tracks. I grew up ignorant of the fact that my respects were long overdue to the traditional custodians of the Gamaragal and I pay my respects to the elders past, present and future.

I'm grateful to my generous readers: Karen Whitelaw, the late Edwin Wilson, Meg Mooney, Jane and Peter Haasnoot and Tracey Dooley, whose feedback was full of heart and so helpful.

I'd like to thank Tony Reeder, editor, who read an earlier version of the manuscript when I was bumbling around in parts of it, totally lost. I'd also like to thank Varuna and fellow writers in 2019 Varuna Memoir Masterclass with Patti Miller. Many thanks to Patti and Dr Carol Major for their professional critiques and encouragement during that time.

Thank you to the enthusiastic Varuna Alumni Zoom Group - Meg Mooney, Dr Jane Messer, Dr Beth Spencer, Madeleine Oliver, Cathy Johnson and others - for their encouragement and support. I'd like to thank Dr Jane Messer and fellow writers for their support during Jane's intensive Bold Ink autumn and spring 2022 workshops.

Many thanks to Vision Australia Library Writing Group; special mention of Writing for Well Being course 2023 and heartfelt thanks to Dr. Sian Prior, our tutor, and to my fellow writers in Vision Australia's Library Writers Group. Thank you to Adrienne Ferreira, True Story Workshop & Masterclass 2023/4.

I'd like to bow down before my literary angel, Karen Whitelaw, for her friendship, guidance and encouragement over many many years.

Thank you to the dear late Stephen Matthews of Ginninderra Press for believing in my first memoir, *Pumpkin,* and thank you to Debbie Lee, new owner of Ginninderra Press, for believing in and publishing this memoir.

Because of the generous contributions by so many, *The Steering Wheel* is now ready for you to take hold of with both hands and enjoy the ride.